Do Whatever Love Requires

Do Whatever Love Requires

Harriet Hammons
&
Carol Ameche

Queenship

Publishing Company

P.O Box 42028 Santa Barbara, CA 93140-2028
(800) 647-9882 • (805) 957-4893 • Fax: (805) 957-1631

Dedication

This booklet is dedicated to God Our Father, to give Him all praise, honor, glory, love and thanksgiving for this booklet, for our very existence, for everything...

For loving us so unconditionally!

Library of Congress #: 97-65317

Published by:
Queenship Publishing
P.O. Box 42028
Santa Barbara, CA 93140-2028
(800) 647-9882 • (805) 957-4893 • Fax: (805) 957-1631

Printed in the United States of America

ISBN: 1-882972-96-1

Declarations

Since the abolition of Cannons 1399 and 2318 of the former Code of Cannon Law by Pope Paul VI on October 14, 1966, in the Decree of the Congregation for the Propagation of the Faith, A.A.S., 58, page 1186, publications about new apparitions, revelations, prophesies or miracles, etc., have been allowed to be distributed and read by the faithful without the express permission of the Church and without a Nihil Obstat and Imprimatur.

In Chapter II, No. 12 of the Second Vatican Councils *"Lumen Gentium"* we read:

> "The Holy Spirit ... distributes special gifts among the faithful of every rank ... Such gifts of grace, whether they are of special enlightenment or whether they are spread more simply and generally, must be accepted with gratefulness and consolation, as they are specially suited to, and useful for, the needs of the Church ... Judgements as to their genuineness and their correct use lies with those who lead the Church and those whose special task is not indeed to extinguish the spirit, but to examine everything and keep that which is good." [Confer - 1 Thess. 5:19-21]

> "Extinguish not the spirit. Despise not prophecies But prove all things; hold fast that which is good. (1 Thess. 5:19-21)

"In cases which concern private revelations, it is better to believe than not to believe, for, if you believe, and it is proven true, you will be happy that you have believed, because our Holy Mother asked it. If you believe, and it should be proven false, you will receive all blessings as if it had been true, because you believed it to be true." [His Holiness, Pope Urban VIII, 1623-44]

It is hereby stated that the messages contained in this book must be understood not as words spoken directly by our Lord and our Blessed Mother, but received, in the form of interior locutions, by Carol Ameche and Harriet Hammons. In accordance with the regulations of the Second Vatican Council, the publisher states that we do not wish to precede the judgment of the Roman Catholic Church in this matter, to which we humbly submit.

Contents

Do Whatever Love Requires

Introduction

"For I am the Lord, your God,
the holy One of Israel, your Savior.
Fear not, for I am with you.
You are my witnesses, says the Lord,
my servants whom I have chosen
to know and believe in me
and understand that it is I, I the Lord;
there is no Savior but Me."
[Isaiah 43: 5,10,11]

All Scripture is inspired by God and is useful for teaching, for refutation, for correction, and for training in righteousness, so that one who belongs to God may be competent, equipped for every good work. (2 Timothy 3:16-17) The teachings and lessons contained in this booklet have been received in the form of locutions since 1988 for Harriet and 1992 for Carol. They are meant to be shared at this time and used by those preparing for, or hearing about for the first time, or having just experienced the Warning or Illumination of our minds to the state of our souls. This event will be world wide, occur at the same moment for every person in the world and be the greatest act of mercy given by God our Loving Father since the Birth, Death and Resurrection of Jesus Christ, His Son.

We focus on the Warning at this point because this booklet is offered as an aid to all those returning to the Father or approaching Him for the first time. It is good to realize that reports of this great gift of God, our most loving and merciful Father, are reported by such Saints as St. Edmund Campion, (1540-1581) and canonized in 1970; St. John Vianney, who died in 1859; Teresa Neumann, a mystic who died early in this century; Blessed Anna Maria Taigi who lived in the 19th century and was beatified in 1920.

God is the Father and Creator of all people, regardless of what each one believes. We are all children of Mary, the Mother of Jesus, as well. There is no truth more important to us at this time than realizing and believing that we are loved by our Creator beyond our imagining.

Our goal is to return to our origin, the Father, with Jesus under the power of the Holy Spirit through knowing, loving and serving the Father, His Will and His Plan. Facing the sin and brokenness in our own lives, we turn with eagerness to the words of Scripture, heavenly warnings, words of love, and promise of graces and forgiveness to all who will repent, reconcile and wish to return with humble repentance, in the love He wants and deserves from all of His creatures.

No one is lost unless they so choose. God is always here for us. His tender love, unconditional mercy and forgiveness are offered for each one who comes in humility and seeks to reconcile with a Triune God Who calls us back to Himself that He might heal us and hold each of His children tenderly, lovingly in His Heart through the Sacred Heart of Jesus, through the Immaculate Heart of the Virgin Mother, our Mother, Mary the Immaculate one who is the Immaculate Conception, who is Their Prophet in the last days of this era which will see its culmination soon. A new era will then begin.

Many of the people of the world have not listened, therefore, are not praying or changing. Evil in the world is only increasing. But hope springs eternal, so we endeavor to return to prayer, meditation and contemplation, as we begin to seek Jesus, to seek holiness in our lives in new found conversions or in our reconversions, and discover that conversion was always meant to be an on-going event in the lives of each person on earth.

This booklet, full of tender words of Jesus and Mary and sometimes the Father, is meant to assist those who pick up their Rosaries to pray, who return to daily Mass and the Sacraments, reconcile with Jesus and experience His profound mercy and forgiveness, begin the practice of daily prayer to prepare for the coming months and years of what we have come to realize as the 'end times.' Our Blessed Mother tells us, life will continue, but differently. There will be many changes in the earth that will include opportunities to defend our faith, the true Presence of Jesus in the Eucharist and Mary as His Mother, Jesus as the Son of God. The time is now for the turning of hearts back to the Father for conversion. There must be no other delays now.

It is Satan who hates God the most vehemently. It is he who hates the Blessed Mother and the power she has been given to share in the mediating of graces and in co-redeeming the world. It is he who began the long history of pride which refuses to serve God. For our struggles are not with flesh and blood but with the principalities, with the powers, with the world rulers of this present darkness, with the evil spirits in the heavens,(Ephesians. 6:12) so we must be always on guard.

II

The Father is Lord and Creator of Satan, also. However, He has an eternal plan for our salvation. He saved us and called us to a holy life, not according to our works, but according to His own design and the grace bestowed on us in Christ Jesus before time began.(1 Timothy. 1: 9) No matter how grim and hopeless anything may appear, we must remember that the power of our God is always greater than that of the evil one and will overcome evil every time.

Much will change in the world, yes, but Jesus, in union with the Trinity will not change. He cannot, since He IS and always WILL BE love, truth, peace, joy, hope for all time and in eternity. We will change because our God loves us so much, He wills to have us change, to come back to Him. Therefore, as any good Father, He will have to show His love through His Merciful Justice, through tough love, through a thorough purification of His world and of His creation, of His people, so that, once again, all will image Him, His love, His mercy, His truth and His light for the good of all.

Our hope must grow in strength and increase our faith and trust in Jesus. A light will dawn. In our souls will flower and blossom Love, true and unconditional love as all have never known or experienced before! We will know the great love our God has for us through this gift of seeing ourselves as God sees us. This is a gift that has never been given to all Their children before, at one time. Hearts will sing with joy and many will come back into the loving arms of Jesus and Mary where each of us belongs now and for eternity.

Every person alive will see the state of their soul. Each one will know there truly is a God. All will be given the opportunity to return to Him and choose for a life of everlasting bliss after a time of repentance and conversion in this life, or a time of making reparation for their sins in Purgatory. Those who do not choose for God will then lose almost all opportunity to convert and return to the Father.

We understand that this event known as the Warning or Enlightenment or Illumination will occur very, very, very, very soon. The word, given to a heart, was reiterated so that we would all realize the importance and seriousness of these words and the shortness of time left. We can repent and return now and visit Jesus in His Blessed Sacrament every day to listen to Him and speak lovingly to Him, asking for the healing of our hearts, so in need of many gifts from the Father. We can pray for peace and conversion for the world. We are called to BE peace and mercy and love to all those who come to us.

III

To develop a personal relationship with Jesus and Mary, will result in ever increasing our faith and trust, growing more every day in Their love and hearts. We become people of joy and hope, love and understanding, peace and patience, all the virtues that are Theirs by Nature for Jesus and gift to Mary. Here is Jesus, the Pearl of Great Price, Mary, the Morning Star, the most perfect of God's creatures. Here is the refuge of the Two Hearts. Here is home, here is reason and sanity, purpose and the end to illusion; here is the fullness of reality and integrity; here is protection and power and strength, fidelity and obedience, (the offspring of humility, says a Saint of old.) Here is Someone Who is for me, with me, calling to me, encouraging me, helping me, interceding for me, waiting for me. Someone Whose agenda includes eternal life and happiness and love for me!

We are never alone, but always in His Presence to the degree that we allow Him. We are grateful for the fact that in one sense He doesn't care what we have done, but only desires us to come back to Him with a sincere feeling of remorse, and repent of our sinfulness. We continually strive to abandon ourselves, remain totally focused on Jesus and surrender of our lives and actions to Him through the heart of Mary. Praise Jesus for our holy Mother and all the events of her life, for her Immaculate Conception, all that she is to me now: mother, example, source of grace, friend, companion, mediator, co-redemptrix, all that is mentioned in the litany extolling her virtues.

Scripture is always our first guideline for this way of learning and living holiness. Contained herein is a framework for understanding and responding to, in a deeper way every day, the love of Mary and Jesus, the Father and the Holy Spirit, to dispel anxiety and frustration; give us open hearts to allow Jesus to continue to work in us. May we give thanks and praise for our resounding good fortune and blessings! May the Spirit of God enlighten and strengthen each of us to persevere in all of our resolutions and new found life in Him that we may come to know the love of Christ that surpasses knowledge, so that we may be filled with all the fullness of God. (Ephesians 3:19)

The meditations from various Saints have been received in the form of locutions (interior) in order to complete the plan to include reflections pertinent to each chapter. We praise and thank the Father for all these gifts to all of you, His children.

We request that you read each section slowly, several times before going on to the next. Also, one is encouraged to return to these lessons and meditations and teachings as a means of nourishing our minds, hearts and souls with spiritual food.

Do Whatever Love Requires

The Day of the Lord

LETTER FROM OUR LORD JESUS CHRIST

"This is an open letter to all Our children of the world from your Jesus, from your Triune God and from your Mother Mary who is here to join Me in this letter to all as a preface to Our lessons and teachings which follow this:

"Dearest little ones, all of you are so dear to Our Hearts. Please know We love each of you very much. I would like to tell you about that love now. I am going to base it on My word in the letter from John in Holy Scripture. You can find it as I will indicate at the end of this dialogue with you. We have chosen the title for this booklet to be, "Do Whatever Love Requires". What does this mean to you? How does it speak to your heart?

"Love is a gift from God. If you had not received this from Him when you became His child, you would be walking, stumbling around in complete darkness. GOD IS LOVE. I am Love for I am God. Love has always been and is meant to always be! Love, if it is in you, dwells in you as a peace that the world cannot comprehend because, on the whole, love does not exist in the world. The world, My people in it, has been blinded by what Satan would have one believe to be love: the material, the self, not caring and sharing with each other love.

"As Scripture says, 'Let us love one another because love is of God and everyone who loves is begotten of God and has knowledge of God...' This means, loved ones, that love is not to be kept to oneself. It is a gift to be shared with others and given back to others and to Me. When a gift (love) is kept, it then becomes a possession. This will have a tendency to lead to selfishness, self centeredness, pride and all the dark side of what the world wants you to believe, and becomes what love is by the standards of the world.

"Again as Scripture has it, 'the man without love (true, unconditional love) has known nothing of God, does not know Me, for God is Love'. As the Father and the Spirit and I are One, We are Love manifested in each other, as We bestow this love to all of Our children. Through Me, the world, My children, should have come to know this love of God because the Father sent Me among you at My first coming. I dwelt with you! I took on flesh and human nature. I became one like you in all things except sin.

"**As Scripture further states, 'Love then, consists in this: not that you have loved God, but that He (God) has loved you...' We love as not one of you can imagine because Our love is Divine. But the Father wanted to show this love to His children who have never really understood what love was. So He sent Me, His only Son, as an offering for your sins. If God can and did do this for you, can you not do this for one another, for Him? Remember, God is Love and anyone who abides in love abides in God and God in him, and that is the way to bring love to perfection.** This is possible for all Our children, as this means doing 'all that love requires'.

"As you meditate on Our lessons and teachings that follow this letter of Mine to each of you, you will see, if you allow your hearts to control your senses and your minds, you will see with the eyes of your hearts what it is We have given to each of you from the beginning of time and how you should be handling these gifts that each of you has received from the Father.

"Yes, each of you has received special gifts just for yourself, fashioned and molded by Him, your Creator, as He knows your need. It is now your responsibility to respond to these gifts if you wish, for the greatest of gifts is love. If you remain in Us, you have love and become love. Look deep within your hearts, My loved ones. Find Me. Find My Mother. For when you truly want to seek Me out, you will find Me. It is not very difficult, as I continue to seek you out. I am at this very moment, as you read this, knocking at the door of your heart. Listen carefully and you will hear My call.

"Close your eyes now and withdraw to that special place in your heart that is Mine, and there I am. You have found LOVE! If you as yet have not made a special place for Us in your hearts, your souls, My love urges you to consider doing it now. If you still cannot because there are so many obstacles in the way, pray, My little ones, for this grace and then go on to the lessons of love which We give to each of you for your growth in spiritual love and maturity.

"If you meditate on this and then find Me, The WORD, in Holy Scripture as We suggest in every teaching to Our loved ones, there will no longer be a doubt that you will have, for you will have found Me, you will have found Us. You will have found LOVE!

"Open your hearts now, please, before you go on to Our teachings, as Our Holy Spirit wants to enlighten each of your hearts and minds as to what We are saying to you on a personal, individual level, just for you and you alone. We want you to know your God loves you so very much now, unconditionally, no matter what you may think, no matter what the world is trying to tell you. We want you with Us NOW and for all eternity.

"COME, COME INTO MY HEART NOW, through the door of Mary's Immaculate Heart and she will take you by the hand, as only a loving mother knows how to do, and will bring you into that refuge of My Sacred and Merciful Heart where miracles are wrought. Once there, I then prepare you to meet your Creator, the Father of all in Heaven, the Almighty and Glorious One.

"You must try to do as I am asking, My little ones, as soon the Father will, through His deep love and mercy for you, allow each of you to see yourselves as He sees you: the condition not only of your souls, your sins, but how you love, how you love each other, yourselves and how you love Him. He will also show you how you did or did not show this love and give it to others, sharing it with His other children around you.

"Oh, My little, little ones, My Heart pleads with you now to accept all I have to give you, all My Immaculate Virgin Mother has to give you through and with her heart. If you feel you are unworthy or this cannot happen to you, you probably are right because you are all sinners. The one who loves and admits he or she is a sinner and asks for Our forgiveness, repents in love, mercy and gratitude, is forgiven. You are completely forgiven because of Our undying, unconditional love for you. There is no sin that is too big not to be forgiven, if you ask. If you do not ask for this, you will not receive this forgiveness and will probably doom yourself to eternal darkness instead of Eternal Light. How can you, as you read this, even consider not wanting to be in Our Light now and forever?

"So come, My little ones, all of you, come back to Me now with all your hearts and souls, your very beings in your hands outstretched to Me, giving all to Me. Oh, how I have waited for your coming back to Me and will continue to do so until the end of time. Learn from Me. Learn from My Mother. Learn from My Joseph. Listen to your Angels. They want so much to help you in this journey back to Us. Then, little ones, dialogue, talk with Me and to Me. This means prayer. Pray, pray and then listen. Listen in the silence of your hearts, as I take you to realms you cannot even conceive, but which are available to you for the asking.

"Yes dear ones, Heaven can be and is here on Earth. FIND LOVE AND YOU FIND ME. Then you have found Heaven here on Earth. When you find me you will have a taste, a look at what is waiting for you and what it will be like in Eternity with all of Us. I love you. I need you. I want you with Me. Come! Come now and journey into this booklet of Ours which can heal what you need healed. Ask Me for this, to convert and change your hearts even more, to show you the Father, to show you Who I Am and what My love has in store for you. I urge you to do this NOW, to prepare yourselves for the NEW ERA to come and to prepare your souls to meet Me one day. Prepare too,

My loved ones, for My Second Coming among you. Some of you will live to see this in the New Era of time which is before you and which is to come soon.

"Surrender all to ME. I leave you with and give you My special peace, joy, hope and love, love and more love. As you finish reading this letter, you are being blest in much abundance and in wonderful and mysterious ways with the grace that will be needed for your special journey back to Us.

"I now say good-bye to each of you. My love is yours, NOW and ALWAYS. Remember, 'Open your hearts to love and then do what My love will ask. Trust Me, for trust is love and mercy.' Do all for the honor and glory of God the Father." (Scripture reference: 1 John, 4: 7-21)

*"God never meant us to experience the Retribution,
but to win salvation through our Lord Jesus Christ,
who died for us so that, alive or dead we should still
live united to him. So give encouragement to each
other, and keep strengthening one another, as you
do already. Be at peace among yourselves. And this
is what we ask you to do brothers: warn the idlers,
give courage to those who are apprehensive, care
for the weak and be patient with everyone."*
[1 Thessalonians 5:9-11 & 14]

THE WARNING OR ILLUMINATION

Blessed Mother: *"My dear children, soon you will see
your hearts and souls as God sees them, as I see them.
Please confess and reconcile now, for the time has come.
You must come back to Him now! You must be in the state
of grace at all times. Regular confession is so important,
dear ones. Sin, any sin, will hamper the grace that He
wants to give each of you. This is the time of trial, of peril
and of change. Many will be confused at what they will
see and hear. Some will not believe because of hardened
hearts. The evil one will be out in a force as strong as the
mightiest ocean. Heed my warnings and stay in the safe
harbor of my heart.*

*"Those who will have a conversion, a change of heart,
will be needed to counsel the confused, those who long
have been away from Our Church and now want to reconcile with Him and with themselves. There will be much
confusion, frustration and yes, much joy. For a time, all*

will seem at peace and that there need not be any other reason to continue in the preparation of their souls and for their continued conversions. This is how Satan will try to deceive even the elect into a passive attitude, a false peace. He will try to convince them they no longer need to pursue this new found conversion.

"This is where you, My chosen, must be ready to do combat spiritually, to confront the enemy head on, to take care of those souls that We will give you. Please, dear ones, help Us with them. Keep them focused on Him, on His Cross. Keep them following only Jesus, My Son, through me and with me through all the heavy deception from the evil one. The evil head of the Anti-Christ will surface soon after this enlightenment of all your souls and then you will see all hell loosed upon Earth and the final battle for souls. Too many, unless strong of faith, will not survive without a strong, courageous faith and trust.

"You must always carry your rosaries, your scapulars, little ones. Use your holy water frequently. Pray for all. Pray for yourselves and your loved ones. Faith will be needed. Peace and love will be needed. My gentleness, wisdom and understanding will be needed and a complete, unalterable trust in His Sacred and Merciful Heart, in His Love and in His Truth, all through me. Keep holding my hand. Your Angels will surround you like never before. Pray with them constantly and unceasingly. Your hope, trust and faith will be rewarded when the new dawn comes.

"These periods will be short, but will be a devastating time. Then will follow the Triumph of Our Hearts to be felt by everyone and light will fill every area of your

world with Our love and peace. Please my children, de-sire to be holy and to be Saints. We want this for you. Come to me. I love you."

Jesus: "Children of My Merciful and Loving Heart, the time scheduled by the Father to show each of you the state of your souls as He sees them is about to unfold. This will be a time of great grace and mercy, for His mercy is love and justice as well. Be prepared now so you can help others when this time comes. Help My shepherds, too, for some will be confused as to what to make of what is happening in souls, hearts and minds.

"So many will be lost because they will not serve. Satan will be out in force to collect all these souls for his own. My Light will continue to shine on each to show what awaits you if you refuse this moment of mercy. Satan, the ruthless enemy, now has in place his army on his battle ground, but we will overcome. All the Angels are in readiness to help do battle for souls.

"The battle is intense even now and will intensify. Do not hesitate to be on guard at every moment. Stay in constant prayer and close to My Heart through My Virgin Mother. Do not lose heart, My dearest children. Never again will there be such an event in the world. Pray with Me, with each other constantly and for each other, and then draw on My strength and My courage.

"The time is here for the Kingdom to come. The time is now for My Father's Will to be done on earth as it is in heaven. Blessed be the Name of My Father. Blessed be His Holy Will and His Divine Justice. Blessed be My

Mother who mourns and weeps for her children at the throne of My Father. Blessed are all those who pray unceasingly for the salvation of the world. I long to take this people of Mine into My arms and calm their fears. Tell My people of My great love and eagerness for the love of them. Tell them that I await the return of My lost ones of the house of Israel to the Home of My Father, where they shall be greeted with open arms and welcomed like the long lost sons and heirs they truly are! I am your Lord Who loves you dearly.

"It will be Our love that brings you all to a new day, to a continued faith in Our promises and to a continued understanding of the events which will follow. On the other hand, it will be your faith and trust which will enable Us to lead you to the truth and to the patience you will need to wait for the fulfillment of those promises. It will be necessary for you to wait patiently for His Will for each of your lives and for your lives collectively."

LETTER FROM OUR BLESSED MOTHER

"Dearest children of the world, I, your Mother, the Immaculate Virgin Mother of the Son of God and My Son, Jesus, am here now to tell you of my endearing, everlasting love for each of you, as did My Son in His letter to you. We want all of you in the folds of this love of Ours: the love of the Father for all the children of His creation.

"We speak of love because We want to dispel any fear that may be in your hearts at this time. There is so much out there in your world that indeed is frightening from one day to the next. There too, are so many prophesies that have come from every corner of the world; some, yes, from Us and some false prophecies not from Us. This is why We need to enforce how much you are loved, how much depends on your prayer to and with Us, in order to keep what should be a normal balance in your daily lives and to try to drive away the evil that is invading and permeating everyone today.

*"Loved ones, you are all so dear to Me and I watch over each of you in the tenderest of fashions. You are protected, (if you wish to be) under my mantle and are in the refuge of My Immaculate Heart. There will be things, there are things now, happening in the world which most will not understand nor comprehend. **It will be hard to justify, at times, love in all you will see, in all you will experience.***

"But, there is Love. There is a great deal of love and mercy in all that is to transpire in each of you and for all of you for the good of all the children of God. That is why this booklet is being authored now by My Son and Myself.

It is to reaffirm and to reassure all Our children of this wonderful, unchangeable love and mercy We have for each of you. We cannot change you or your thinking. Only you can do this for yourselves. We can only suggest what We know is best for you and for the good of all humankind.

"We cannot interfere in your free will, but We can urge you to reconsider how it works in your life and how love plays a part in this life of yours and with those around you. We then can supply, through Our various chosen instruments around the world, what We know are the necessary tools you will need for the todays and for the possible tomorrows to come.

"I plead with you most urgently, most lovingly and tenderly, to take to heart Our words found in this little booklet. We feel with the grace you will receive, in any change you wish to make in your hearts, in your life styles, that you will be strengthened by Our love through this grace to understand many things, and then to be able to cope with any and all situations that will present themselves to you and to the whole world.

"Please, go now, as you read this, to Holy Scripture, My loved ones, to 1 John in chapter 4 and read from verse 17 through 19. Pray about these words inspired by the Holy Spirit and ask Him to open your heart to what these words will mean to you and for you. There is not now, and will not be in future days ahead, room for fear....fear of any kind. Fear is not from your Heavenly Father. Only love is from Him. That is why We have impressed you with Our deep love, Our concern for your well being, Our mercy and Our compassion for each of you and for Our entire world.

"Because of this love of Ours and what We hope will be a love returned by you, you will receive the grace to cast out all fear by calling on Him Who is Love, Jesus, by running to me, your Mother, for consolation and for protection, and to the Holy Spirit for guidance and direction and the grace to live as was always planned for each of you, and for the grace to be used for anything that may be needed by you in a particular circumstance or at a particular time in your lives. Please take these words to heart from this Scripture, those from Jesus and myself and those you will find in this booklet, and then pray continuously for what I have suggested you do.

"I love you deeply and enfold you in my motherly arms and kiss each of you most tenderly now and always. I am and will be always a prayer away. Come to me, let me love and nourish you and fill you with His love."

Do Whatever Love Requires

Chapter One
Reconciliation

MEDITATION FROM BLESSED FAUSTINA KOWALSKA

"Dear ones, Jesus taught my soul many years ago, that when you go to confess your sins, you must have a sincere desire to repent and make up; to reconcile for these sins and then truly be sorry. You should be determined to strive for sanctity always in an effort to reconcile with your Lord. If you are not open and sincere in all humility when you come to confess your sins, you put yourself at risk of not benefiting from your confession. It is important to remember that the priest is only there, sitting in place of Jesus himself; that it is Jesus you are talking to, so if you let pride linger in your soul you are kidding only yourself, as Jesus knows, and you have not helped yourself to make a good confession. **You must be honest with yourself and with your confessor!**

1. A soul must have complete sincerity and openness.
2. It must be humble and it must be obedient.

When a soul has done this with its confessor, it will then have made a good confession and will be rewarded by a strengthening of its faith. I send my love to all God's children, letting them know I am praying for them and with them. **Call on me to help in any need!** Call on any of the Saints, they want to help all in their journey to Heaven."

"For whoever wishes to save his life will lose it, but whoever loses his life for my sake and that of the gospel will save it. What profit is there for one to gain the whole world and forfeit his life? What could one give in exchange for his life?"
[Mark 8: 35-37]

RENEWAL

Blessed Mother: *"The Father begins now to lower His hand to strike the earth, to strike the heel of weakness of His people in order to fashion them anew. He has only love for all of you. He will be fashioning and forming the earth and its people in His Image from now on. Keep remembering that this is what is happening, as you view events about to unfold. The day and the hour are upon the world. Kneel in readiness and be prepared for all that is about to come. Please, My little ones, believe My words and be filled with peace. This peace is the love of My Son and my love.*

"The Father would never allow His little ones to suffer without the help of the Angels and Saints. Call on their help at any time. This does not mean that all will be saved from suffering and dying for their faith. Incredible hardships will begin any moment, and I beg you to remain in constant prayer that each will receive the graces offered. Each one will realize that their decisions will depend only upon the individual. The knowledge that God has written on each heart prepares a person to accept the graces offered. It is a choice we make alone, devoid of the influence

*of others, and **that must then be lived out in spite of the choices of others or their future decisions.***

"Please, receive the Sacrament of Reconciliation as though you might not have the opportunity again. Give your attention to My Son and Myself. Live now in Our midst and count on all the help you will ever need. I am the Immaculate Virgin Mary who waits eagerly, as well, to begin the final battles. Much will be accomplished and then again lost. Perseverance is the gift all of you must offer to the Father during these times. As you are more purified, the conviction will become stronger to remain faithful. And as you pray and serve, your purification will become greater!"

Jesus: "These times are rich with My Father's gifts, My little ones. More people need to know that they are available to each person who comes to Me seeking forgiveness. This, children, is the key to releasing all of the gifts stored up for every person since before their birth. All have the opportunity to be renewed by My hand if they will only ask My forgiveness and pledge to Me their sorrow and eagerness to repent. It is a humble act to beg. It is a saving act to beg forgiveness for one's sins and confess them to Me.

"My people, the Kingdom of Heaven is worth any sacrifice, any suffering in order to render one ready to approach the gate. I am the Gate. I am the Narrow Path. I am your All, your only means to salvation through the Heart of My Mother and power of My Spirit. Let your heart be consecrated and dedicated to Me, My dear ones, in the Holy Trinity. If you will retreat and renew yourself, you will find all the strength you need waiting in My arms.

The power of grace to overcome temptation and struggle is victorious every time you ask for it. Come to Me more often, dearest ones of My Heart. You can know the battle is accelerating when the fight becomes more difficult. The struggle against evil can be nearly overwhelming and frightening, too. You see why trust in My Mother's protection and My strength is so important. Just remain in the shadow of My Cross, resting now in My arms. Lean on My Mother.

"Loneliness is meant to bring you into My Presence, accepting all the love I wish to give you. Vulnerable is a condition that can change when one's motives are humbled and purified. All can be tempered by penance and fasting. When you offer all things with joy, great strength, (My strength), will take their place in your heart. Weakness, children, is meant to alert you to the need and areas of healing that must be offered to Me and then requested in trust. The Divine Will of the Father is *that all of His children be purified.* You hesitate to surrender to the death you must endure to all that is of this earth. Please, My dear people, rest in My embrace and heal.

"Dear children of My Heart, you must forgive. Go back to the table of the Lord, work together for the good of all and not the few. Many need to see how mercy can work in their lives. Mercy needs to be lived and should be practiced in your lives by forgiveness. All My people need My healing touch which is My mercy and love. This I give most effectively through My Sacraments of Reconciliation and Eucharist. This is the time for Reconciliation, for new starts, as there will be fewer opportunities because of the adversary working his deception in many to such a degree as to have them believe what he is saying and doing.

"Nothing happens unless I allow it and want it for your growth to reconcile, to open eyes and hearts to see your own pride. I then give each the choice to repent and start over. I pray with all of you that you come to Me to ask for forgiveness and then to forgive each other. Do not give me or each other any more lip service, as I know what is in hearts and how sincere you are. Come to Me please, dear ones, in humility, obedience, and trust in Me for forgiveness. The time grows short. You need to love as I love and forgive as I forgive.

"How sad it is that so many have the sin of pride and refuse to fight it. You give in to the world, to various gods like your own pleasures, your self centeredness, and listen not to the voice within which is pleading with you to come back, to repent and come into My Arms, to My Heart, your only true sanctuary from the evil that is all around you.

"Come often to My Sacrament of Reconciliation my children, even with the slightest sin, as this is a sure way of grace, of showing Me that you have contrition and repentance and it is from your heart. NOT ONE SOUL DO I WANT LOST. Come to Me in My Sacrament of Love and reconcile with Me, with your neighbor and with yourselves. Once a soul has rid itself of all excess baggage, it then can get down to basics . . . that of LOVE. This is why a good, sacramental confession is so important."

It is a world filled with sin.
It is a world filled with greed and self-destruction.

It is a world content to allow madness to rule and do nothing to change things for the better.

It is a world filled with its own need, mindless of the need of My beloved poor and starving children ... starving for food and for the light of Christ.

It is a world where chaos rules the hearts of godless men who fear nothing and no one, but their own fear of loneliness and emptiness."

REPENT AND RECONCILE

Jesus: "The Lord, your God, is waiting to receive you into His love, into His fold, so that He may shepherd you and bring you back to the one true Church of Jesus Christ. I love you, no matter what you have done. I need for you to come back to Me and love Me. I NEED YOUR LOVE. My people, I wish for you to be united to My Sacred Heart, where you will be healed, but you must spend much of your time in prayer and remorse with Me, your Physician, much like you would spend time in a hospital being healed of physical wounds. Your wounds are deep, and time is short! Please, spend all the time you have with your Beloved Doctor Who longs to bind those wounds with His love. Please, have all the assurance you can that you are forgiven when you come to Me to be reconciled. Please, children of the world, reconcile with your God before it is too late. Reconcile with each other and forgive each other ... NOW. This is a time for strengthening, a time for storing graces and My blessings for the days to come. Great will be the darkness. Great will be the turmoil and panic.

Reassure and guide the people and help to keep them from being frightened, for great will be the fear.

"My people, I wish for you to understand how very short is the remaining period of time, as you know it. Would that I could delay My hand, but I am unable to because of the many and great sins of mankind. They no longer believe in Me, or care that I call them back to the harbor of truth and unity of faith. EVENTS WILL MOVE QUICKLY, AND OUR PEOPLE MUST MOVE WITH THEM. THERE WILL NOT BE A GREAT DEAL OF TIME LEFT IN WHICH TO REPENT."

Blessed Mother: *"Man must learn to honor his God and to listen to His commandments. Until the earth is cleansed of sin, there will be much weeping and gnashing of teeth. The hearts of many will be broken, and men will return to God with remorse. I weep, so often, tears of blood for My children who will be lost. Many will still be saved because of the prayers of My faithful ones. Do whatever you can to spread my words to all of our children. Do whatever you can to encourage all to pray without ceasing.*

"Know what comfort is there with My Jesus. Please, be warned of the shortness of time, the little time that is left to repent and convert. The Sacrament of Reconciliation is the place to begin. A new day will dawn for all to see who will turn and be faithful to My Son. How quickly you must return to your Father's house, lest you die of wretchedness and hunger. Prodigal ones will truly be like sheep without a master. They must return to the one fold and one Shepherd.

Do Whatever Love Requires

"People will die because of the great destruction, and those who are worthy will be purified in the fires of Purgatory. The prayers of many are needed to purify the souls going into eternity. These times are most serious, and call for the unity of all My children on this earth in order to offer one prayer of petition to the Father. He is greatly saddened by the need for this punishment. He does not wish to destroy, but only acts as a last resort in the face of a stubborn, stiff-necked people. The end of time, as you know it, My dearest people, is near and your Savior calls, but with great sadness and a heavy heart, 'Come back to Me, people. Time is running out, is gone, and your Lord and God can no longer hold back His arm of vengeance."

"Dear ones, I your Mother of Sorrows speak this night for the benefit of your hearts. Please listen closely to My words. They are given as pure gift from the Father Who made us. We are His creatures and He loves us all so dearly, so totally, so invitingly. He invites us to approach His throne with joy and cry out 'Abba'! The beginning of a deeper relationship with Our Creator is one of deeper simplicity based on our littleness.

"His great Fatherly love for us is meant to make us comfortable in His Presence, to relax in the warmth of His care and wonderful providence for our lives. In these times of terrible chaos and destruction of lives, each of you needs, more than ever, to know your God as more than approachable, as the One Who directs every action around you for your good, to bring you most quickly to Him."

"Put to death, then, the parts of you that are earthly: immorality, impurity, passion, evil desire, and the greed that is idolatry. Because of these the wrath of God is coming [upon the disobedient]. By these you too once conducted yourselves, when you lived in that way. But now you must put them all away: anger, fury, malice, slander, and obscene language out of your mouths. Stop lying to one another, since you have taken off the old self with its practices and have put on the new self, which is being renewed, for knowledge, in the image of its creator."

[Colossians 3:5-10]

DYING TO ONESELF

Jesus: "Dear children of My Sacred and Merciful Heart, in today's world it is so important to completely die to oneself, so I can truly live in a purified you. Your soul then will be ready to accept My Kingship over all that you are, that you do, that you think and say. You are then wholly Mine and I am wholly yours and you have learned how I AM THE TRUE WAY, the true and only Life, the only and most honest Truth that has ever been.

"To enter My Kingdom it is very important to have Me and to have the Holy Spirit of God, that We may live completely in your hearts, your souls, in your lives. There is not one facet of you that We do not want to abide in, but cannot unless you have rooted out sin, all desire of the flesh, all faults, and have replaced them with the virtues. You have to die completely to your old selves, the self that loves things in and of the world. To be in the world, and not of it, is something all should strive for. By grace to die to self, (obtained through prayer, sacrifice and disciplining yourselves) you will experience a gradual fading away in your lives of wanting and doing this or that. The material things will no longer have a hold over you. You will want to pray more, spend more time with Me in the Blessed Sacrament, receive Me more frequently in the Holy Eucharist. You will nourish yourselves completely with Me, living wholly for Me and in Me. This must be done every day.

"Die to the flesh and live according to the Spirit. There has to be a decision made by you to do this, to unite yourselves, your wills with Mine every day and then pray, pray, pray that the Holy Spirit will shower you with the graces of His gifts. Ask for all of them, and He will give you what He knows you need and what He wishes to bestow on your soul. He will let you know what needs working on, and then you are to work on it. Listen to Him. Pray to Him.

"My dear ones, there has never been a greater need in the hearts of man, as there is now, for the Holy Spirit to work in each of you. Let Him consume you. Let Him guide and direct you. It is only then that you can be mercy, can give mercy and can accept mercy. Listen well to My Words! It will not be easy because the world, the sins of the flesh are so rooted in all of you that you will fall many times. Then get up, cry out to Me for help. Cry out for Me to help you carry the crosses of self denial and self mortification which will over shadow self-centerdness. SELF - SELF - SELF must die! You must live your Baptism of purity of heart, mind and soul. When you find yourself being tempted, come to Me, to My Mother, Mary, and to My Holy Spirit. Satan will not give you rest at these times. He will try his best to show you the futility of it all. Resist him with all that is in you. Call on Us. We are never away from you. Only sin can drive Us away from you. As the days darken more so, Satan and his legions will try every deception, every twist to your very natures to dissuade you from Me. Through grace received as you continue daily to die to self, you will find added strength and courage enabling you to grow in holiness. You will find you have additional armor to withstand his strongest wiles and temptations.

"Those of you who have been consecrated to Me through Mary will have to remember that consecration daily and sometimes hourly, as your trials will now become even more so. But as you resist and call upon your Mother and as you call upon My Name, (the Name that dispels demons - JESUS) you and I will then be walking the same path and you have resisted the wiles of Satan. As this is done, you will truly be strengthening the faith you acquired through your Baptism into My Death and will then start to live in union with My Resurrection. You will begin to see as if you did not see. The eyes of your hearts will be leading you and you will be conducting your heart to control your thoughts.

"*You will begin to hear as if you did not hear*, because then only will you understand the gentle murmuring to your hearts. You will listen and understand what you hear. Even though you still hear what the world is saying and see what it is telling you, the eyes of your heart will be set on Me, on the Kingdom of God.

"I gave you eyes to see but also a heart to see with. If something goes directly to your heart and a change takes place, you become peaceful. You then will be walking with Me and listening with the ears of your heart and seeing with the eyes of your heart. You will use the things of this world as if you were not using them at all. You will have rejected the things of the world Satan wants you to accept. Your focus is off you and back on Me where it belongs. You will have chosen to live with Me, in Me and through Me. You have died to yourself.

"Tell My dear ones how I long to hold them in a warm embrace of welcome. My Father longs for their return, and will dress them in festive garments and hold a banquet for them! Great will be the rejoicing on the day of each one's return. The lost sheep of the House of Israel will one day return and accept Me as their leader and Messiah. My dear ones, beauty can be restored to mankind only after the ugliness is removed! The laws of My Father for His people will be reinstated in hearts emptied of sin. The graces He wishes to shower upon them will flower in the renewed soil and cause beautiful blossoms to bloom, once again, in the Garden of His Will. My dear ones, remain in simplicity and humility, waiting for My Father's Will to act on behalf of the world. NOTHING will happen until He decrees it. But all will occur, as you have been promised repeatedly. You are loved so very much, My people. As you let go of expectations and fears and excitement, you learn to just be in joy and peace and hope in My Father's Will, accepting whatever happens or doesn't!

"It is absolutely necessary for you to be able to live like this in order to live in total union with Me. It was like that for My Mother waiting for all to be accomplished when she knew all of the details beforehand. It was a matter of patient waiting for Me as I traveled the hill country around Jerusalem waiting for the exact time to be revealed to Me. You know how things must unfold in My Father's Plan. It will always be this way, since it is only our Father's Will that is being fulfilled."

"You have been told, O man what is good,
and what the Lord requires of you:
Only to do right and to love goodness,
to walk humbly with your God.
[Michah 6:8]

PATTERNS

Jesus: "My children, please come to Me in faith and trust, letting go of all pride, anger, ego, self; all the hurts and faults, the "I", and I will heal you. Give Me your hearts, hands, eyes, everything, for there is nothing I cannot do. Surrender that very last drop of self to Me and see the miracles. Your God is servant to you because of My over-whelming love for you. Not one soul do I want lost.

"Come to Mary often because through her, as Mediatrix of all My graces and being the Spouse of the Holy Spirit, she is a Mother that wants all of you to know, love and serve Me, as I do you. She loves with a love not compre-hensible. She loves with My Love. We are One and Our Hearts beat as One. There is nothing I refuse My Mother when she brings it to Me. She brings all your needs, your weaknesses, your faults to Me. She does not judge. She loves and helps each of you on that path to holiness, to Heaven. She is the perfect model of how one dies to one-self. Follow her example. Pattern your lives after her. The Holy Spirit wants to give you this grace. Accept it and it is yours. It is a treasure untold.

"You need to become little in My Eyes, so I can give you the love that I want to share with you. To become little is to die to self each day, every minute of the day. You then can truly respond to this love of Mine as a little child in trust and in complete abandonment to Me, to what I Will for you. When you are small in the eyes of the world and have become like little children, I can then mold you and shape you into models of Myself and of My Mother's Heart. I can do many wonders in each of your hearts and souls.

"As grace flows steadily from My Heart to yours, miracles are wrought, souls are saved and then nothing is impossible. If more of My children understood how much I have to give, how far reaching My love and My mercy are (always has been and always will be), you would then understand much.

"You must become small, nothing in your eyes, in the eyes of the world, so I can become your strength, giving you graces through My Mother, as the Mediatrix of all Grace. This you will need in order to live in holiness, to become like Me and to prepare yourself for Sainthood and for your Eternal Home in Heaven. You are Mine, all who are small and little in the eyes of the world and in worldly thought. You have become giants in My Heart and in the Heart of the Father Who loves you.

"Read My Holy Words in Scripture every day. As I feed you through this, meditate on The Word. Ask Me, ask My Holy Spirit to enlighten you as to the meaning of what I am saying to you through the Scriptures. Give all, including your distractions, to the Holy Spirit and He will give you an abundance of grace, understanding, wisdom and discernment. These lessons are given to purify you, to help you know how to be emptied of all self: self centerdness, self esteem, self worth. Me, Me, Me or I, I, I is then taken out of your beings and replaced by Myself through grace and by the virtues you will need now and in the days to come. Be always in My Peace. LIVE MY WORDS!

"Now, I want to go a step further in what My daughter St. Margaret Mary had to say to all of you regarding charity and humility. I will include her thoughts with Mine for the conclusion of "Dying to Self.""

St. Margaret Mary: *"Conform yourself as closely as possible to His humility and gentleness in dealing with your neighbor. Love those who humble and contradict you, for they are more useful to your perfection than those who flatter you. We must endeavor to the utmost of our power to enter into the adorable Heart of Our Lord by making ourselves very little and humbly confessing our nothingness, thus losing sight of self entirely."*

Jesus: "All must work on loving those who humble and contradict you. I know it goes against every fiber in your bodies to be humbled in such a manner. It is a means for your perfection. It is a means of mercy. As you remain focused on Me, on My Cross, you will see how being humbled and contradicted for My Name will bring you closer to holiness and to perfection.

"My children, you who strive for holiness in a complete dying to self, must be courageous and must be strong in not giving way to depression because of faults or the humiliations you encounter each day. For some this will be a difficult lesson. My wish is for all of you to persevere and call on the Holy Spirit for the grace you will need. He knows when you need something and how to help you, as long as you are open to Him, to being purified, to being corrected and open to change. Children, when you have lost sight completely of self and you are no longer holding any feelings of resentment or anger, you are learning to be meek, humble and gentle as I Am, being submissive to Me, to My Love and My Mercy. Much grace is given a soul who learns this lesson.

"You are to bring all to Me through Mary's Immaculate Heart and through My Holy Spirit. When you give Me full rein, you then will be purified at all times so you can radiate My Light to this darkening world. This is a MOST IMPORTANT LESSON TO LEARN and one that is difficult for the human nature."

The following is recommended:

- Matthew 16:24 to end of Chapter:
- Matthew 13:10-23:
- Colossians 3:1-17:
- John's Gospels, all of Chapter 12
- St. Margaret Mary quotes - "Thoughts & Sayings of St. Margaret Mary."

Do Whatever Love Requires

Chapter Two

Prayer

MEDITATION FROM SAINT JOSEPH

"Beloved children, Our God, the Father, Son and Their Holy Spirit, has asked me to speak to your hearts about prayer. Children, you are all mine, those of you who wish my patronage, my protection, help and heart to heart advice.

"I used trust throughout my life on earth with prayer to God. When given the responsibility to care for and protect Jesus and Mary for the heavenly Father, for all of you, I saw to it that our lives centered around prayer. We prayed the Holy Word which you now know as the Bible or Holy Scripture. This was the foundation of our lives for the growth of our family in holiness.

"We, my Mary and I, taught little Jesus throughout His growing years all we knew of what was written in the Torah, in Scripture. Every good Jewish person had knowledge of what our God was saying to us and we imparted this knowledge to God's Son, our Son, Jesus.

"Soon He was teaching us as He was teaching those in the Temple. His wisdom and ours grew through prayer to our Father. We relied much on God the Father because we believed all that was told us by Him. There was a trust, a bond in faith that continued to grow in our small family. We loved. Oh yes, we loved each other deeply. We loved the Father and Creator of all. We loved our neighbor and kinsmen. We even loved those who meant to do us harm.

"Through prayer, complete trust and faith with wisdom became the seat of the holiness we were experiencing in our little family. We relied and expected all from our God. We worked, all three of us worked. Both Mary and I taught Jesus many things and as we were to find out later, He began to teach us many things.

"Through prayer all things were possible in our family, in our day to day lives. You will find dear children, that this is still so in your lives. If you only realized the merit and the many benefits and the knowledge you acquire through prayer, you would never stop. This is especially so with prayer in the family.

"I would urge all families to come to a heart decision to pray more openly with each other, with Us as the Holy Family and with our God, the Father, the Son and the Holy Spirit. You will find as you do more of this, you begin to open your hearts as He wishes all His children to do. Oh the progress you will then make in holiness, as you mature in your prayer lives.

"I am not telling you there will never be crisis or problems facing you, either personally or in the family, but it becomes easier to accept because you know you have God where you want Him, and exactly where He wants to be...in your hearts, in your lives, and in your homes!

"I love you. I am your Joseph who will protect and defend each of you when called on, as I did my little Family and as I continue to do with those who ask and pray for me to come to them."

"Now to him who is able to accomplish far more than all we ask or imagine, by the power at work within us, to him be glory in the church and in Jesus Christ to all generations, forever and ever. So be imitators of God, as beloved children, and live in love, as Christ loved us and handed himself over for us as a sacrificial offering to God for a fragrant aroma. Immorality or any impurity or greed must not even be mentioned among you, as is fitting among holy ones. Come, then, we will make a pact, you and I; the Lord shall be a witness between us."

[Ephesians 3:20-21 & 5:1-3 / Genesis 31:44]

TRIANGLE OF LOVE

Jesus: "My littlest ones, it is most important to be able to help Me help other souls on their journey to salvation. Increasing holiness in your life through graces given will help in the preparation for the salvation of your soul and others. Souls: yours and your neighbors, must be your goal.

"Remember "THE TRIANGLE": God at the top, Who is the focal point. In one corner of the triangle, your neighbor and in the other yourself. Your neighbor is everyone-your families, both biological and spiritual, everyone in the world. Their souls are important, as are those souls who are in Purgatory. When you do not step out of this Triangle, you cannot be centered on self, because your FOCUS is first on ME, your God, then your neighbor and then yourself. I can work miracles in anyone who will remember this. I am then completely and wholly One with you and your 'self' is no longer your prime concern and focus.

"My little children, please read and meditate on Psalm 51. I will create a clean heart in those who wish to have one, a heart that will belong to Me alone, a soul purified to a degree of being ready for anything; either to come to Me for all Eternity or, if I Will it, to stay and fight for My cause in the battle for souls between the powers of light and darkness.

"Come back. Please come back! Adore Me! Praise Me! Pray with Me and to Me! Love Me! Put Me back in your churches, your lives, your hearts where I belong. Did I not suffer and die for each of you so you could be with Me and I with you for all time? Won't you show Me the respect that I your God, your King, your Savior deserve? You who will still come and kneel before Me, acknowledge My Presence, please pray for those who have become so tepid and lukewarm. Come to Me in adoration. Worship Me, those of you who have put Me first in your lives, then pray, pray for your wayward brothers and sisters."

Blessed Mother: *"My precious little ones, as you sleep, you can ask your Angels and Saints, as well as those holy souls in Purgatory, to continue your prayer from the day so there is never a minute without prayer that will be ascending to my heart and to the Throne of the Most High. What joy the soul has who knows me and knows My Son. It pleases Us to do everything for that soul. Continue to always pray for conversions, for sinners and for those who do not seem to want to accept Jesus. You do well to say* *continuous Rosaries and Chaplets of Mercy for souls who seem lost and those who are on the brink of perdition. Help Us help them, your bothers and sisters. Continue to strive each day for holiness and to pray for souls. I, your Mother, love each of you tenderly."*

> *"For this reason I kneel before the Father, from whom every family in heaven and on earth is named, that He may grant you in accord with the riches of His glory to be strengthened with power through His Spirit in the inner self, and that Christ may dwell in your hearts through faith; that you, rooted and grounded in love, may have strength to comprehend with all the holy ones, what is the breadth and length and height and depth, and to know the love of Christ that surpasses knowledge, so that you may be filled with all the fullness of God."*
> [Ephesians 3:14-19]

FAMILY CONSECRATION

Blessed Mother: *"Dearest families of My Immaculate Heart, families should come to me so I can help them know My Son. Come to me for faith and trust. Come to me and accept my love which I hold in My Immaculate Heart for you and for every family. All families must bond together, more closely than ever, because there will be a great tide to try to separate them. I refer to all families, biological and spiritual. Prayer leads to peace in families. When you do not pray together or cannot, then each individual must pray for them for the grace to understand the value and the importance of this grace, this gift that is communication with their God and Creator.*

"Please children, consecrate your family to the Holy Family asking this Holy Family to intercede, so yours will become holy and one as They are. They are The Family

each family should be patterned after. Family here means your biological family, but there are extended ones as well. There are communities of religious, there are parish and diocesan families, there are single families. There are spiritual families and The Church, His family, the Body of Christ.

"At special times of the year such as Christmas, all should try to do this consecration together in love to His Sacred Heart through My Immaculate Heart. [e.g. "Total Consecration..." - St. Louis De Montfort.] This consecration should be done with a pure heart and with love. It is so important to be in the state of grace. To make a total consecration of a family to His Sacred Heart through My Immaculate Heart is a commitment."

Jesus: "Dear ones of My Sacred and Merciful Heart, We are now coming back to reclaim that which is Ours and We need your help. We cannot come to a soul unless it says 'yes.' We are here to help sanctify and elevate the family to the status of My Holy Family (when I came to earth almost 2000 years ago); to teach all to model their families after Ours; to pray together; to have God the center of all they do. Then once again peace will be restored and the Reign of My Sacred Heart along with the Immaculate Heart of My Mother will smile on each of Our children.

"When you consecrate your families to My Sacred Heart through Mary's Immaculate Heart you immediately gain strength, courage and the grace to persevere in the moral and holy standards I continue to set before all of you. This will give you peace and love. A new prayer life in your family will evolve. I will give you gifts untold and

graces you will need. All families who consecrate themselves to Me must renew this family consecration often,
together and individually.

"Pray much for your families as this is where I inspire
and instill with special graces the young, the parents, those
in My holy families who pattern themselves after the first
family: Jesus, Mary and Joseph. Keep holiness alive in
your families through prayer and encourage the young to
consider the religious life. From these ranks will come the
next generation of Saints who will lead all in the next Millennium.

"My children, no family would exist if it were not for

Me, the Father and for the Holy
Spirit. Virtues, morality, holiness, love are being stolen from
you by the deception of Satan.
My Mother comes to help you
to help Us restore Our rightful
place in the center of all families. Listen to her, please. I love
you and bless all My families in
very special ways."

PERSONAL CONSECRATION

Blessed Mother: *"Dear children of My Immaculate Heart,
when you have consecrated your hearts to Jesus through
My Immaculate Heart, your responsibility to Us begins
and increases. Jesus and I take all of you: your bodies,
your souls, your hearts, your works, all that is interior and*

exterior as well as those whom you consecrate to Us. The door that opens directly to Jesus' Sacred Heart, to His mercy, love and grace is My Immaculate Heart. It has always been that way and shall continue to be. That is why it is so necessary, so very important that more know of consecrating their lives to Him through me. This is no longer an option. It is now a necessity!

"Dearest ones, when one is consecrated to Jesus' Heart, through and in My Immaculate Heart, you can go out fearlessly doing the work which will be expected of you. You will never be alone. As you consecrate to me each day your entire selves, you will receive graces and blessings to be able to do in wisdom and courage what needs to be done each day for us. I also invite all priests, bishops, religious to consecrate or re-consecrate themselves, their parishes, their dioceses to Jesus' Sacred Heart through Consecration to My Immaculate Heart, praying for the Triumph of My Immaculate Heart with the Reign of His Sacred Heart to come soon.

"I am your Mother and I will take care of all who are mine, who are consecrated to me, to Jesus. The mark of the Beast will not touch them if they but give me even a small part of themselves. This makes it possible for me to work His grace in their beings, their souls and hearts which will lead to their conversion. Your fiats [saying 'yes'] are important to be joined with mine, so I can place them all in My Immaculate Heart and give them to His Sacred Heart as testimony that you now belong to me. Through My Heart many doors open in the Kingdom. So come, come and partake of all the gifts that await each of you."

Jesus: "Dear ones of My Sacred Heart, it is most important many more are consecrated to Me, through Mary, as it will herald in the *Reign of My Sacred Heart and Mary's Triumphant Immaculate Heart.* It is now time to stop doing all the things that take you away from Me.

"It is well you ask My Mother to always give you her spirit to live and breathe in you. You will need her courage, her gentleness, her attitude of peace and love so she can work My plan in your lives for the salvation of all souls. Remember, when you do all with her, in her, through her and for her, you are doing it with Me. Her heart and Mine are one and when she has joined your heart to hers,

 you become one with Us. *All must know of the love Our Servant Hearts have for all Our children*, and how from Our example and the living of your consecration, you will learn to be as We are: One with Us and with each other, as the Father always meant it to be."

"Rejoice always. Pray without ceasing. In all circumstances give thanks, for this is the will of God for you in Jesus Christ."
[1 Thessalonians 5:16-18]

PRIESTS

Blessed Mother: *"Dearest children of Our Hearts, I, your Mother, would like you to continue to join me, join all of Heaven in prayer with Jesus to the Father for Our loved priests, bishops, religious and Our most beloved Pope. This century has seen many changes in their lives which have taxed them to the limits of their humanity. My children, you cannot exist without Our priests. They are the ones who bring Jesus to you through the Consecration at the Holy Mass. Each of you needs my sons, and they need you. Will you continue to join me and all of Heaven in prayer for them? Please keep them close to your hearts. Support them and love them as so many are overworked and wounded.*

"Yes, there is apostasy, dissension and division in Our Church, but these will not overcome His Church. Prayer, love, and mercy in all forms will overcome any and all obstacles in Our Church and with my loved sons and daughters. Pray with me unceasingly, day and night, letting them know you are praying with and for them, that you support them and the truth, as handed down from Jesus through His Vicar on Earth. Nothing is impossible through prayer.

"Pray that all dissension, apostasy, division and disunity will cease so all will once more be united as one under Our beloved son, Pope John Paul, and what he

29

teaches you from Us. Be on your guards constantly as Our adversary will try to dissuade you from praying for priests and religious because he despises them. He hates them because they represent Jesus on earth. Bring all to Us, to Our Sacred Hearts, for refuge in these troubled times. Keep peace, joy, mercy and love in your prayerful hearts for these much loved sons and daughters, as well as for each other."

*"The Advocate, the Holy Spirit that the Father will
send in My Name, He will teach you everything and
remind you of all that I told you."*
[John 14:26]

HOLY SPIRIT

Jesus: "Dear ones of My Sacred and Merciful Heart, with
the Spirit's special anointing of your hearts and minds,
many graces and gifts are given to you. He wants to bestow on you a continuous stream of gifts, fruits and virtues. As you receive the gifts He gives, you will increase
in virtue and the fruits will be evident.

"Come always to Me and to the Holy Spirit through
Mary's Immaculate Heart. She is Our Love. The Father
chose her from the beginning of time to be My Mother, to
be your Mother and to be the Blessed Spouse of Our Holy
Spirit. As you go forward in love, keep the Holy Spirit
close to your hearts with your constant prayer of Consecration to Him, to My Sacred Heart and to the Immaculate
Heart of Mary."

Blessed Mother: *"My dear children, the Holy Spirit comes
to those who keep their hearts open, trouble free, with no
thoughts or desires beyond what He wishes to give. Do not
get too busy with the world. Stay in quiet with me and with
My Son so you will be able to recognize the voice of the
Holy Spirit and to receive the gifts He wants to give you.
You need to pray continuously in your heart for the grace
of His gifts which He has to give as well as the direction
and guidance for your life.*

"In these days it is important you listen to hear Him. Listen in silence, in prayer, and then do what is being asked of you. The Holy Spirit will continue to speak to a heart which is open to hearing Him. Carefully heed what He tells you. Rely on your Angels to direct you on the path to find Him. Pray with them and to them. Talk to them. Keep close to me and to the Holy Spirit for continued guidance and direction. Satan is out in fury and will try to deceive you. We are here to help.

"Beware! Do not let pride in! Do not think you can do this on your own. Only with Our help and through the following of your heart with His indwelling will this happen. Look to me always. Run to me, to My Immaculate Heart and there you will find shelter. Seek me. Seek Him and you will find what is necessary for all your needs, your doubts, your misgivings, for growth in holiness.

"Children, you will be given much for perseverance in humility, obedience, charity and love, but know too, much will be asked of you. Pray to the Holy Spirit each day for His enlightenment, His discernment, His grace for the virtues you will need for strength and courage, focused on the Cross and on your crosses."

STAND FIRM

Jesus: "Dearest children of My Divine, Sacred Heart, see how some of the candles on My Altar in My Presence, (this was during Eucharistic Adoration with tiers of candles on the altar) are burning so much faster than the others. I liken these candles to a soul, to a heart. Some have many fervent intentions of what they will do and then go at it too fast without stopping or thinking. This is what I would say to all of this: You pray hard, work hard, do everything too quickly and sometimes do them very well while in My Presence, but while in prayer, whether in My Presence here in adoration or by yourselves in My Presence, all has been done too fast, with no thought and usually not in real prayer. Before you know it, flames have gone out (fervor); you have lost your enthusiasm, your drive, your want and need for Me and for prayer.

"Then look at those who, like My candles that burn slowly, ponder and reflect on Me, on My words, on My Will. They meditate often and slowly absorb what it is I am asking of them, telling them and blessing them. My children need to slow down so their flames do not go out, but rather flicker gently as I Will them, not as they will. They need to be in silence with Me, in the silence of their hearts and minds to ponder, to know, and then live My Will. There is no other way to find Me, to find My Will for each of your lives. What more could you possibly want or need? Am I not sufficient to supply you with everything? PRAY...FAST...SACRIFICE...Give everything over to Me, to My Mary, so that I indeed can live wholly and completely in each of you. I need you, My dear ones, so much to be Me, to be My mercy, to work in My Divine Sacred Heart and Will; to let My light of love and mercy shine to all, so all who see you (as the flickering candles), see Me.

"Pray often for My son, Pope John Paul who is always in deep prayer for all of you. You cannot imagine the weight he carries for you his flock, My children. The world situation weighs heavily on his heart. His is a mission that no one else has. He has the weight of the knowledge of things to come. Please increase your prayers and increase prayer groups. Pray intensely because the evil one is deceiving many and causing division. He is creating havoc in all kinds and forms of crime, crimes of the flesh, crimes against My little ones, the littlest ones not yet born. Oh how I cry for these who are being murdered in their mother's wombs.

"Remember, the Mass is the primary prayer with Communion, followed by the Rosary. These done in the purity of your hearts and in the state of grace can stay events and put a stop to some catastrophes. Adore Me, praise Me, thank Me for everything. Let Me know I am God and that I do play an important part in your lives; that I am at the center of your worlds, your very beings.

"Come to Me to be filled. Help Me fill each vessel that comes. I will do the rest. I plant the seeds through you and then, as doors open, My grace and mercy can penetrate through hearts and souls. Nothing is impossible for Me for I and I alone am your God! Put yourselves completely in My Hands and Heart My dear ones, in faith and trust each day through Mary's Immaculate Heart and you will see transformations take place. There will be miracles and I will be the Center of all who come to Me.

Do this only one day at a time, each day. Stand firm on faith, hope and trust. Be strong of heart, mind and will, spirit and feelings. I am here always for you my loved little ones, I love you with a love that will never cease and is not comprehensible."

Blessed Mother: *"Sweet ones of My Immaculate Heart, pray with one heart and mind in unity with the Holy Spirit, in union with Jesus and myself at all times. I invite you to give me your spirits by rejection of them and to ask for my spirit and my dispositions. Ask for my thoughts, desires and feelings. Say often the prayer to 'Our Lady of Good Counsel.' I will guide and direct each through this prayer, as I counsel you."*

Prayer: Mary, I renounce my spirit and I ask for your spirit. Mary, take away my thoughts and give me your thoughts. Mary, take away my desires and give me your desires. Mary, take away my feelings and give me your feelings. I am totally Yours and everything I have I offer You, O my beloved Jesus, through Mary Your Most Holy Mother. Come Holy Spirit, come by means of the powerful intercession of the Immaculate Heart of Mary, Your well-beloved Spouse. (Then say three Hail Marys repeating after each, 'Mother of Good Counsel, give us good counsel. Amen.')

"Souls are precious to me, to My Son, Jesus. We want all to be saved. Please continue to pray, to be in His love, to invoke His mercy, my mercy. We intercede before the Throne of the Most High God for all your intentions, for all the intentions of holy souls who pray for Our inten-

tions. Your prayers, sacrifices, fasting and good works are being united with my prayers for the salvation of souls and for the conversion of many. My prayers are always united with those of Jesus. The Father refuses the Son nothing, as My Son refuses me nothing.

"'Praise to the Father, the Son and the Holy Spirit.' This should always be on your heart and lips. Praise and thanksgiving are the sweetest sounds to ascend to the Heavenly Throne. There need be no words to do this, just a lifting of your heart, uniting it with mine to His and let it soar as on the wings of a bird, as a dove. As you progress in prayer, invoke the Holy Spirit to be with you, then He will dwell in special ways in each heart and will give you the graces necessary for your needs and will give guidance and direction on your path to holiness.

"Pray for your country. It is in most serious and grave danger. Unless it comes to its knees and pleads for forgiveness and repents of its heinous sins against God and Our Sacred Hearts, there will fall a judgment, a merciful judgment that will be felt in every home, town and state of yours. You must pray for the world. It is so far from Our Hearts, from God's love and mercy and only the people of the world can change this tragic situation.

"So many false prophets tickling ears, as they are telling the world what it wants to hear. The world is not listening with its heart. Pray, O pray for all my children, all who are your brothers and sisters of the world and who are in the world. My children of the world have forgotten how to pray as I have taught them for so long. Pray that the eyes of hearts will be opened, especially those who are not listening and living what I have been teaching.

"Remember, your guardian Angels love to pray with you. Invite them more often. The Saints in Heaven love to join their prayers with yours. Invite them too. All the choirs of Angels pray when asked to join you in prayer. Their songs and prayers are glorious notes taken to the throne of God. It is all one song of praise and thanksgiving at all times: Gloria. Gloria. Hosanna in the Highest. What joy this gives the Father's Heart. Pray night and day. All night vigils of prayer are most important. Eucharistic Adoration vigils are the best kind of vigils. This appeases the Heart of Jesus and God the Father.

"Please, my children, I would invite as many as can to hold three day and night vigils of prayer and fasting, preferably in front of the Blessed Sacrament, or in your homes, invoking the mercy of the Father on His people through Jesus. I will be praying with you as you do this and I will send many Angels to pray with you. Give all these prayers to Jesus, to me, so We can continue to plead to the Father for you, for the world.

"Advance in your prayer lives, especially through prayer in silence before Him when in adoration of Him. When you receive Him in Holy Communion, it is then that the silent prayer from your heart of praise, thanksgiving, joy and love touch Him most and fill His Heart with your mercy. He loves it when He and you are united in Communion and are wholly joined in love and mercy. My loved little ones, praise, thank and show your love to your Heavenly Father always and in everything you do. I love you with my mother's heart and will always be here for you."

> *"First of all, then, I ask that supplications, prayers,*
> *petitions, and thanksgiving be offered for everyone,*
> *for kings and for all in authority, that we may lead a*
> *quiet and tranquil life in all devotion, and dignity."*
> [1 Timothy 2:1-2]

JOY & HOPE

Jesus: "You can show the Father the depth of your desire by doing all in your power to prepare yourself. In the near future, your prayers will be answered if you will completely dispose yourself. The action must be twofold...one on your part and one on the part of God, Our Father in Heaven. Please dear ones, also pray for the strength of greater endurance and surrender. Persevere in joy whatever He sends you. The number of souls who are affected and saved will be limitless. The trials accompanying this time will be also limitless. Only a deep trust and total unity with God's Will for each person will see you through each development.

"Please, trust that all will work for the glory of God and the salvation of many souls, especially when it looks most hopeless. The impetus to pray and prepare is a sign of grace and favor! The Spirit of Wisdom and Truth will come to your aid every time you call upon Him. You may believe this and count on His help completely. He will not let you down, I promise. It is His Nature to be Wisdom and Light to all who call upon His help."

Blessed Mother: "*My dear ones, please be aware of each crisis which develops in the world, and pray for mercy on* *those who are suffering now, that they may be urged to respond to the call of their God which comes in the midst of the storm. Be aware of the countless who suffer and die in each corner of the globe, and offer them to the Father for His mercy and forgiveness.*

"The love We have for you is boundless, My children. Please allow this love to flow through you and out to all you meet. It is in this way you will touch more and more those We send to you. It is not easy to look beyond the feelings and attitudes of others, but you must learn this important lesson and practice unconditional love and gentleness. It is only love which can melt the hardness of Our children's hearts.

*"Pray to the Angels to help you and remind you each moment to offer all to Me, and I will purify each thought, each act, and carry your pleas to My Son Who awaits your love and service with great eagerness. **Each trial is a treasure being stored in Heaven for your return!***

"Persist in love and truth, My dear ones, and know again of My constant love and protection. I am your loving Mother. Hearken to these words. Pray as you have never prayed before, and be filled with love and joy and a fierce determination to hold out till the last moment of time that is left in this Age. You will see unbelievable events and wonders worked by the hand of My Son. At the last possible moment, I will be victorious over the forces of evil, and Satan will be crushed and hurled into the burning pit!"

"With all prayer and supplication, pray at every opportunity in the Spirit. To that end, be watchful with all perseverance and supplication for the holy ones."
[Ephesians 6:18]

PRAY AND RETURN

Blessed Mother: *"I, your Mother, wish for you to practice praying to me and thinking of Me at every moment. You will be calmed and quieted in this way, my children. You will be molded and formed into my image very quickly if you allow me to be present to you at all times. My presence will change you; will strengthen you and will keep you close to me and My Son. Please try again and again to do this, as it will be very difficult to accomplish. But with practice and the help of Our Holy Spirit, you will make great progress.*

"You are seeking a greater union with Me and that is the first step towards acquiring it! Continue to practice inviting Me to be with you and pray with you at each moment of your day. I long to hold all My children in My arms and welcome them into heaven where they belong! Hearts are growing so tender and so dear as you pray and spend more time with My Son and me in the quiet of your heart. Remember the most important duty is that of prayer and living in the presence of your God. With this awareness, a new peace will descend upon you, and you will go from one task to another with ease, making of each one a prayer to offer to the Father."

Jesus: "My dear ones, you must spend more time in silence before Me and allow Me to heal you. AVOID ALL THAT WOULD DISTURB YOUR SPIRIT FOR YOUR OWN SAKE, and dwell in Me in My Sacred Heart! You are safe in the silence of My Presence, have no fear. Please, continue to tell Our people of Our great love and longing for their return.

"Follow My Mother; listen closely to her, for she will bring you to My Sacred Heart each moment of the day. Be united with her in prayer and love. Allow her to be your teacher and guide. Stand by her in the dark days to come. Be a beacon of truth for all who will seek Me. Bring Our lost ones to her and, together, bring them to Me. I await you in My Blessed Sacrament. I long for My children to return to their Lord.

> In the warmth of the smile of My Mother, all is well!
> In the shadow of her Mantle, we are favored.
> The love of My Mother will bring mankind to their
> knees to honor and adore the One, True, Living God.
> It is My Mother who will bring the lost sheep back to
> the fold.
> It is she who loves Me so much and soothes the grief
> I feel for My lost ones who reject Me.

"Follow her manner, children. Learn from her gentleness. Be still and listen to the soothing tones of her voice, the melody of love which sings from her heart. Be aware of the gentleness with which she accepts all who come to her, how she calms fears and tenderly wipes away tears.

Do Whatever Love Requires

Go with Her into the depths of sorrow within each heart that comes to you. Listen quietly and patiently as they pour out their stories of sadness and loss. Give courage and strength to Our dear ones in the Name of My Mother and Me. Assure them of the ease with which they will be received by the grace reserved for them since the beginning of time. Comfort them with the trust in My promises which is theirs for the asking."

Chapter Three

Holiness

MEDITATION FROM SAINT THERESE, THE LITTLE FLOWER

"These words I give are for the people of the world who are seeking to return to the Father in humility and repentance. I am Therese, the Little Flower of Jesus, Our loving Lord, and I come to bring you great joy and love and peace. His Majesty has allowed me to speak for the good of all the dear ones who love Him and attempt to be more closely united to His perfect Will.

"As you know, the little way of perfection was always most dear to my heart. There is no other way than purity, simplicity and living with a humble heart when one wishes to serve the Beloved One. The tiring things we do everyday in the life of routine and service while on earth, are powerful opportunities to build a mighty edifice of love for our dearest God. The Son, Who loved us to His death and obeyed His Father in all ways, has shown us how to unite our present situation to His sufferings. He lived in such poverty, pouring Himself out in every act of kindness and obedience. He never questioned His life or living conditions or the fatigue that accompanied the rejection and ridicule of so many in the world at that time. He traveled without any of the normal comforts and as a human, suffered all the emotions and feelings that accompany the harsh treatment of others. He bore all of this with love and patience, my dearest brothers and sisters.

"When I was a sister at the Carmel in France, I was never able to travel far to serve the poor, or to fight the evil one's intentions for the souls of my comrades in prayer. We were a poor people compared to the people of this Age, and yet the Divine Master allowed me to offer whatever I had to give in order to perfect my soul and be of help to others and serve their needs. It is really simple, but your world, especially, needs to slow down and be made to experience its poverty without the sustaining hand of God's gifts for a short period of time. This will be, so that all will be forced to appreciate the little things and realize their total dependence on their Creator.

"You will have nothing soon to call your own. It is then that I invite you, my dear comrades in Christ, to invite me to show you how to build your spiritual life out of nothing! Because, to have nothing allows us the opportunity to have all. To do without, to slow down and pray, to see yourselves as dependent on the Mighty hand of the Father, will bring each one to the realization of His great love and devotion to His people.

"Oh my friends in Jesus, how I wish there were time to tell you more. However, the ability to be little and humble in the eyes of each other, will bring freedom and true joy to your hearts. And your hearts, little ones of Jesus, is where you will find everything you need, everything you wish to offer for the good of all. You will discover the Kingdom of God's Will where I live already surrounded by all of your Saints and Angels, too. The Holy Mother

Mary is here and Jesus Who allows me to speak words of love and encouragement.

"Be little for Him, and I will help you. I shower roses of humility and joy upon each of you as you read. I send my great love for Jesus into your hearts at this moment. Please believe that I am very near to you and ready to help you enter the New Era of peace and holiness. Be of stout hearts and filled with gratitude at the great gifts being offered to those who return to receive the love and forgiveness of God Our Father with humble hearts, with glad hearts, with all of the littlest duties you perform for each other as the greatest stars in your heavenly crowns. I will be here for you, I promise, praying and sending my love, my roses of joy. Thank you, thank you for listening. I praise the Trinity in union with the heart of Mary, the Immaculate One. Adieu."

> *"Be sober and vigilant. Your opponent the devil is*
> *prowling around like a roaring lion looking for*
> *[someone] to devour. Resist him, steadfast in faith,*
> *knowing that your fellow believers throughout the*
> *world undergo the same sufferings."*
> [1 Peter 5:8-9]

VIGILANCE

Jesus: "It is most necessary to live in an environment of gratitude, as this leads to greater humility. Within each one of you lie the seeds of virtue, which only need to be desired through prayer and exercised with diligence and patience. Please, continue to seek humility and simplicity, My dear ones, and the days will see an increase for your progress on the path to My Will for you. The very desire to do the Will of My Father is His gift to you. Please remember to offer each task to the Father and then thank Him at the completion of each one. If you live in this way, you will be living in the presence of God and all His Heavenly Court, the nearest to Paradise you can be on this earth.

"You fill My grieving Heart with joy, as I watch you struggle for patience and holiness. Please continue to struggle against your sinful nature. All will be accomplished, little ones. Your purification is continuing according to the Will of My Father. There is great rejoicing over all My dear ones who pray and strive to do His Will. When pride is discovered, it can be offered to Me for healing and thus, conquered a little more! All of these discoveries are necessary, My dear ones, to further purify you in order to serve Me in a greater way. The Kingdom of God, My children, is worth fighting for!"

Blessed Mother: *"The dawn of each day will bring a need for greater awareness of the need to consecrate each word, each conversation to the honor and glory of God. This will increase your awareness, and sharpen your protection against proud words of conceit or boastfulness. The tone of voice with which we speak to each other can, indeed, be healing or hurtful. You have no wish to harm anyone, my children, I know.*

"Yet, without constant vigilance, old habits can easily creep into your behavior. Be alerted and on guard by the knowledge of the ease with which these former ways of being are waiting to trap all of you and pull you down. Fight with all of your might against the wiles of the enemy. He is ever active against those who love and serve me. There will always be this residue of sin which clings, which allows each of God's children to find some small or even large smudges, signs of sin, to be cleansed. The important thing is to continue to try to discover the roots of personal sin and bring them to My Son in the Sacrament of Reconciliation. My dear people, the ability to be humble and obedient will be your greatest assets in the coming days. Please continue, My little ones, to come to My Son more and more.

"The patience you practice, dear little ones, will be invaluable in your future. All who live will see the saving power of God. Many will be healed of ailments to give them an opportunity to repent and pray for themselves and their lost loved ones. A New Day of Grace will dawn for all who are willing to accept it. This next time period is so very critical to the salvation of Our beloved lost ones."

> *"For this very reason, make every effort to supplement your faith with virtue, virtue with knowledge, knowledge with self-control, self-control with endurance, endurance with devotion, devotion with mutual affection, mutual affection with love."*
> [2 Peter 1:5-7]

VIRTUE

Blessed Mother: *"My dear little ones, without virtue it is difficult to have mercy and love. Continue to pray to the Holy Spirit for my virtues, for my spirit to be yours. When the Most Holy Trinity sees a likeness of me in someone, there is nothing They will not do for that one according to Their Will. This is always for the salvation of a soul, for the crowning of a soul in Paradise where the soul will one day see Them face to face. Please continue to stay with me, joining your Fiats every day with mine to be taken to The Father. This is the way He can continue to mold you more into His Image and Likeness, as you imitate me and my virtues.*

*"My patience with my children is endless. This is what I would like you to learn from me: **my patience, my humility, my obedience, my charity.** I would like you to pray to imitate these virtues of mine. Until you do this, you will not know what and how I feel or think, and I want you to so much. When you pray for perseverance in humility, obedience, charity and love, know you will be given this according to His Will for you. Also, know then much will be asked of you as well.*

"Pray to the Holy Spirit each day, on the hour if necessary, for His enlightenment, His discernment, His grace

for the virtues you will need. Pray to Him for strength and courage and to strengthen your faith and trust. Keep focused on the Cross and accept the crosses you will receive from His Mercy and Love. It is important you pray and work closely with the Holy Spirit. His gifts will prove invaluable to a soul. My virtues, the virtues He endowed me with from the beginning of time, are important for all to have or you will not be able to remain calm and in my peace at all times.

"The Holy Spirit works in wonderful, mysterious and wise ways, and only the heart and soul who is in communion with Us in silence and peace will be able to hear Him, to be able to receive the grace of virtues of which everyone is so much in need. He wishes to give in abundance these virtues if you ask. He will answer according to what He knows is your need at a given time.

"I am The Holy Mother of all virtues. I am here to help those who want to grow in holiness and virtue. Imitate me, and many graces and virtues will be yours. As you pray to the Holy Spirit for this, you will begin to walk in the Light of My Son, Jesus. There is such a lack in the world of the virtues, especially in your country. I am coming again in many places through His Power, Blessings and Grace to help all of you realize the gravity of the way you are going. Please help me, little ones of mine, so together we can show others how to live, once again, virtuous lives.

"Slow down in your ways of doing things. Seek me. Seek Jesus more often. Rest with Us and speak to Us. We have all you need. Lean on Us. Trust Us. Have faith and confidence in Us. Love, trust, faith and prayer will overcome all ob-

stacles. When you practice the virtues you need, you will see self vanish gradually, and the 'self' that needs to die will be replaced by the virtue that is needed. The prince of darkness loves those who center on self and forget the virtues. With the practice of virtue you will find the path to holiness easier."

Jesus: "Beloved children, practice the virtues of My Holy Mother. Follow her example always. Listen to her in all things and listen to the Holy Spirit Who will descend on you as He did at the first Pentecost. You will then receive His gifts. Some will be different from others, but I tell you, ask for all of them and their fruits which are the virtues: the virtues that Mary had all her life and which she now dispenses with the Holy Spirit to those who seek them.

"You will know the gifts, graces and virtues that are coming to you, as you live your lives with the Holy Spirit and with My Holy Mother. I beseech you not to hesitate ever to accept them, as all this will strengthen your hearts and wills to be Mine, so no evil can penetrate the fortress of grace We will build around each of your hearts and souls. Give all to Me through Mary Immaculate, as she is with you to lead you in the holiness of her virtues on that path of holiness that leads to Us in Eternal Life."

"Do nothing out of selfishness or out of vainglory; rather, humbly regard others as more important than yourselves, each looking out not for his own interests, but [also] everyone for those of others. Have among yourselves the same attitude that is also yours in Christ Jesus."
[Phillipians 2:3-5]

HUMILITY

Blessed Mother: *"Dearest children of My Immaculate Heart, humility is a precious virtue. It is a love virtue filled with mercy for your God, for me, for each other and for yourselves. When you have humility you are blest, you are holy as He is Holy. Where true humility of heart exists, He is always there, for there is no longer any sign of pride of any nature. You have then died to yourself. You no longer have your ego to contend with, the 'self image'. You are righteous for God. Your resentments and judgments fall away completely, as then you see others as I do, as the Trinity sees them, as children of God. No matter how difficult this may be, you must be able to control and put aside your feelings about people that are negative and ask yourself how Mary, how Jesus sees them. How do They love them? And then act towards them in that manner. Humility is the virtue I wish all would strive for and work for the most. Humility is to be meek and humble of heart in all things. Look to My Son's Heart, to my heart and seek refuge there in Our Hearts. Learn from me, your Mother who wants to teach you everything there is to know to please Our God."*

Jesus: "My littlest ones; learn My Virtues. Please give Me your hearts and accept My humble and merciful Heart because of My deep love for all of My children. Through humility and charity, you will find a sure path to dying to one's self, to abandoning all to Me, to giving up your will in favor of My Will. You learn to acquiesce to those things which would normally go against your very nature.

"You must love in all mercy, Me, yourselves and each other. When you look at a person, look with the light of love which is charity and mercy because, as you look into the face of a brother or sister you are looking at Me. *If you cannot see Me you have not died to the world, to self.*

"You must learn to conform yourselves to My virtues of humility, gentleness, charity and love when you deal with others. When you are thusly formed you need to heed these lessons and then your hearts will truly be in union with Mine. You must not stand affronted when some reject or humble you, for if you accept it as I would do and as I did, you will learn a great deal more on how self dies, much more than when someone flatters you. Flattery, pats on the back are not in the lesson on humility and dying to self. They add to pride, and pride is contrary to humility. Pride is a complete contradiction of humility, charity and obedience. Pride is a great enemy of obedience. Heed these words of Mine.

"You must learn all this, as this is what My Beloved Mother Mary has been teaching you for a long time. Work on it every day. Pray and meditate on it. Take it into your heart ever so seriously and then pray the 'Chaplet of Humility' every day from now on, along with the Chaplet of My Divine Mercy. Oh the graces you will receive from doing this and how more like My Heart will your heart become."

> *"Everything is lawful, but not everything is*
> *beneficial. Everything is lawful, but not everything*
> *builds up. No one should seek his own advantage,*
> *but that of his neighbor."*
> [1 Corinthians 10:23-24]

PRUDENCE

Blessed Mother: *"Dear children of My Immaculate Heart, one practices the virtue of prudence by trusting and by listening to the Holy Spirit, not by acting rashly or impatiently. With prudence, caution is recommended. Both prudence and caution should be exercised. This then is called a holy caution and prudence. Many good judgments come from prudence. There are many who think they are being prudent. It is sometimes being overshadowed by enthusiasm. It is not wrong to have enthusiasm, but one must, with the use of prudence, as with enthusiasm, sit back and wait for prudence to dictate to your emotions.*

"Emotions so many times, as many have found, have been dictated only by enthusiasm, by rejection or by frustration, worry or by fear. Fear destroys hope. How many negatives, as well as positives, are being dictated to your beings, to your spirits, which come in the form of an emotion? It is wise, as My Jesus teaches, to take all of this to Him, in front of Him in His Real Presence and present to Him your very self; giving Him through me all these feelings, these emotions, whether negative or positive, good or bad, and then wisdom and prudence will come instead of an adverse emotional feeling not built on His grace.

Do Whatever Love Requires

"When one seeks prudence, it must be done diligently and not in haste or in worry or fear because of what others are saying or doing. One must always come to Us for Our judgment, Our discernment, whether it be something you feel you should do or not do, or someone whom you feel is to be with you or not. Your spiritual self needs to rid yourself of all the world and what it thinks. It is so even when you seek direction in anything.

"Your heart, your spirit must be at peace, a peace with and in Us. Then joy and holiness will seep into the spirit, into your heart and it will negate, through grace, any negatives that are trying to take over; even the positives that are not from God."

"Thus faith comes from what is heard, and what is heard comes from the word of Christ."
[Romans 10:17]

WISDOM OF FAITH

Jesus: "My beloved children, what is wisdom? What is faith? You ask Me to teach you, to enlighten your hearts and minds as to what is meant by Wisdom of Faith. First, you must see from your heart and understand that all wisdom comes from the Father, from the Triune God. Wisdom is not something that can be acquired like a new pair of shoes or a bag of groceries. No, wisdom comes from Our Hearts to your hearts.

"To possess faith is to have discovered a great treasure. It takes prayer, prayer for the grace to be able to have this wisdom which enhances and builds on your faith. Faith, as you know, is not something that can be given through the world. Faith and wisdom in the world are but folly. Faith (and the wisdom to know how to acquire this faith) is God given. Our Father has given you many examples of this wisdom: the wisdom which leads to growth in your faith, to a firm, unshakable foundation that will outlast the worst of storms. The examples are many, and are there for you to use wisely. Ask for them. Pray and fast for this wisdom of faith. Look to Me, to your Savior and King, for the highest example of wisdom of faith.

"I have shown you through My life, My suffering, death, and resurrection what you are to do to acquire this treasure and then to live it, to let it shine through you, to pass it on by your examples. It is a gift, the greatest gift of mercy and love which the Father bestows on hearts, on souls who wish to accept this treasure. It is free, but only in the sense that you then go into the world, who is in such darkness, and show them by your lives, by your actions, what it is and what it means to live as one with Us in love, mercy, faith, joy, and hope.

"Listen to Me. Adore Me. Live joy and hope in complete trust and perseverance. Live simply, out of a complete turning to Me through this wisdom. Through this you will find a strengthening an enlightenment of your faith and wisdom which comes from much prayer to Me and with Me through a communion of Our Hearts and your utter dependence on Me for everything. These are important steps in Wisdom of Faith. You need patience. You need trust. You need Me, all through Mary and Joseph. Depend on Me. Die to yourselves, so My Spirit can work in you to accomplish this stronghold of faith."

II

*"For no one can lay a foundation other than the
one that is there, namely, Jesus Christ."*
[1 Corinthians 3:11]

Jesus: "Faith is likened to a castle or fortress which is built on high ground, (surrounded by a body of water) which is impenetrable. It is firm. It is solid. It is strong. The same with faith. This stronghold of faith in each of your hearts and souls cannot be built without the wisdom to know how, when and why it is being built. You need a master architect and builder. I am that Architect and Builder. The price is high: your souls given to Me in the same trust, love, and joy I give to you.

"As I build, I also serve. I wish to have you do the same, to follow My example, My path of light to others. Show them how firm your structure of faith is through this wisdom you have learned and acquired by following My examples and teachings, by following Joseph and Mary and now, also by following My Vicar on earth, John Paul who is the beacon of wisdom and faith. He has complete wisdom of faith.

"The keys are: purity of heart, state of grace, repentance and reconciliation with Me, (with each other and with yourself), the sacraments, which I instituted for your sanctification, My holy Word and the truth which My holy shepherd teaches. He teaches you because of his firm and deeply rooted wisdom of faith. Without this, one will never find the truth, as you will be always blinded by what the world would have you believe is truth.

"This is such an important lesson. It is one which is most simplistic, but one which will prove to each soul the worthiness of this endurance of faith through the wisdom We give to each, when asked for. To accept it, one needs to be an open vessel, one that listens, instead of doing, doing, being busy constantly, as when the Holy Spirit comes, He comes to the silence of a heart, a soul, and He rests there, if welcomed. He cannot stand the hustle-bustle of the world.

"Focus yourself on Heaven through the Cross to My Sacred and Merciful Heart, through Mary's Immaculate Heart, and BE STILL AND KNOW THAT I AM GOD. Remember Mary's words at Cana, which should be burned into each heart, "Do whatever He tells you." You cannot do this unless you wait in patience and trust, knowing I am here. I know when the right time is for you to receive these graces, graces of Wisdom of Faith. I do My part, always. I never change! Now you need to do your parts to become one with Me and like Me.

"You will know when you have wisdom of faith by your love, your joy, your trust and your humility. Wisdom of Faith is likened to a child who rarely questions, accepts in trust, in love, in faith and does all in joy and gladness of heart. My blessings I extend to all My children and I pray that more will seek this wisdom to find the faith that will be so much needed for the ensuing months ahead. This is an imperative requisite for the preparation going into the year 2000. My love, peace, joy, and wisdom, I wish to give to all."

III

*"But as it is written: What eye hath not seen, and
ear hath not heard, and what has not entered the
human heart, and what God has prepared for
those who love him."*
[1 Corinthians 2:9]

ST. JOSEPH ON WISDOM OF FAITH

St. Joseph: "Over the years I found the more I turned myself over entirely to my God in everything I did, whether it was in my work as a carpenter or in prayer (silently in my heart or in reading the Torah, the Holy Scripture) or in my going from one place to another, my strength grew inside of me. No, not physical strength, but spiritual strength, so much so that when I was to take Mary as my wife and found she was already with child, I was confused. But as I turned to my God in suppliant prayer, He sent His Angel to calm my fears and my heart. My faith was in Him and I never questioned it. I therefore was learning to become strong in wisdom of my faith, believing all He said to my heart directly or indirectly and never questioning. I was being taught wisdom through a source I knew not, but my trust, my faith, did not waiver because of this wisdom with which I believe He was filling my heart and soul.

"This grace of wisdom, as Saints have found, is a priceless treasure, a pearl of rare beauty that compares to none and should be treasured. When a person, a soul, desires and matures in wisdom of faith, he then is giving all to Jesus in complete trust, knowing through this grace that His wishes far surpass any human semblance of what the world would have you believe wisdom to be. Wisdom led me to complete faith, but I found it was not easy. Wisdom should be nurtured. It will grow and will feed faith, giving you a strong sense of oneness with us, the Holy Family."

Blessed Mother: "*Dear, dear little ones, faith must be built by following whatever the Will of God appears to be at the moment without hesitation and without conditions. Know that the Father's time is not yours, no matter what is said! Know that your docility and obedience to all that does or does not occur is central to your growth into His Divine Will. The only thing necessary for you to say at each moment is 'yes' and 'Amen'.*

"If you are upset by anything, do not be alarmed, My little ones. You are very human! When you bring your emotions to Jesus and to me, We can heal you more and calm your inner turmoil. Trials are just that. They leave one feeling inadequate and puzzled and helpless. They are designed to place the focus on God and His power and show us our own lack of it. When we are completely dependent on God for all things, we will experience this in a huge way, so that we cannot miss the fact that He is God and will provide for everything."

"Finally, draw your strength from the Lord and from his mighty power. Put on the armor of God so that you may be able to stand firm against the tactics of the devil. In all circumstances, hold faith as a shield, to quench all [the] flaming arrows of the evil one."
[Ephesians 6:10-11 & 16]

THE NEED FOR TRUST

Jesus: "It is I, your Lord, Who am Lord and God of all. There is no other like Me. I am the First and the Last, the One True God. Praised be My Father and Our Holy Spirit. Stay close to Me and My Mother, My dear ones, so as not to be deceived. The evil one will try anything to distract and confuse. Do not give him a moment's attention, but quickly pray and drive him away in My Name. You will be blessed and protected in the Mantle of My Mother. In times of war, the enemy is everywhere. When your battlements are built on a solid foundation, all will be well. There is nothing to fear for those who trust in Me.

"You all must learn more patience and trust in the Father's providence. He has been caring for His people since the dawn of their creation, and always does what is best for you at that moment. Our Holy Spirit is preparing you for a time of chaos and confusion which will tear this world apart! Families will turn against each other. Members of families will mistrust and hate. In order to survive, people will do anything necessary to save themselves and thus, a time of terror will prevail. It will be then that you will need to trust totally in My power to defend and protect you. Have faith and trust in My words, for the time has come for My great plan, the Plan of God, Our Father, to be enacted for the salvation of the world.

"Prepare for the events which are about to begin and will lead My people to the Day of the Lord. On that day, you will see the glory of Heaven coming on a cloud, and your heart will rejoice and sing hosannas! The lion and the lamb will dance in victory over the defeat of the evil one. It will be a long and arduous journey from now on.

"Please ask for the grace of being emptied before you begin to pray. Seek and ask for union with Me every moment of your day. Abandon all of who you are and receive all of Who I Am.

"THERE IS NO MORE TIME. These are warnings of a grave future. There will be no peace to be found, as My churches will be used for other purposes, and My Sacred Host and dishes will be desecrated. No, not forever, but the darkness will be great for a long time and you will be desolate without My Eucharist to comfort and nourish you. You will see the abomination of desecrations upon My holy altar, and you will see the blood of My faithful priests upon My altar as a sacrifice for the sins of their brothers. Great will be the bloodshed and great will be the terror of My poor little ones.

"You must be completely immersed in My strength and the belief that I will never fail you. Many will be counting on you to fill them with courage and faith and point them in the right direction."

"For God did not call us to impurity but to holiness. Therefore, whoever disregards this, disregards not a human being but God, who [also] gives his holy Spirit to you."
[1 Thessalonians 4:7-8]

GRACE

Blessed Mother: *"Dearest children of My Heart, when a soul has reached a certain spiritual maturity by grace, the little pearls of grace given to that soul become most precious and valuable in Our safe keeping store of treasures. Souls are like small children and are to be handled gently and carefully so as not to harm their progress of growth. It takes some a very short time and others a much longer time for this progress to take place. This time span has been planned by the Father before the world began. Each of your souls has special graces, pearls of grace, that are for you alone and no one else. Your soul matures spiritually according to your faith and your complete trust in Him.*

"Each soul has been given a free will, this too being a pearl of grace. If handled according to the plan of the Heavenly Father, the soul will unite itself more readily to His Will which is the ultimate goal for all souls: a complete unity with Him in His Will. This is when the soul no longer cares to exercise his free will, but rather returns his will to the Giver, the Creator.

"I am the Mediatrix of all grace, so I know how to take a soul and show it how to please Our God by giving

it to His Son, My Son Jesus, in complete surrender and consecration to His Mercy, to His Sacred Heart. Once united to Jesus through me, the path is cleared of any and all obstacles to reach the throne of the Most High God, the Father Who loves with incomprehensible tenderness all His creatures.

"There are many souls (because of how the world is programming you in your every day lives) who miss what He had intended and still intends for all souls. As Scripture has said, 'they have eyes, but do not see, they have ears but do not hear.' (Matthew 13:15) They see only what their minds, eyes, feelings tell them and this is usually from the world. Once they have learned the secret to listen and see with the heart, souls will still know and hear what is about them but are listening and seeing with their hearts. Souls are where the Triune Divinity dwells, where I dwell when invited. Then in the silence of your hearts miracles happen, transformations occur, changes take place and grace takes hold of you interiorly.

"When a soul is in the state of sanctifying grace, it is likened to a radiant jewel and it has gained the Kingdom here on earth. A soul in the state of sanctifying grace is a place where the Most Holy Trinity wants to dwell at all times. It is Their special delight because They can come freely through me into my garden in your soul and rest. This gives a soul much peace, joy and happiness which is not describable.

"To be in the state of grace is a treasure because of what the soul becomes in the sight of God. Being in the state of sanctifying grace, you become so bright that the

Angels sing out in loud voices, 'Glory to God in the Highest', joining your soul voices with theirs in praise of God. Your souls become so elevated that, if you could see with your human eyes what the eyes of your heart and soul sees, you would know how pleasing you have become to the Holy Trinity. All of Heaven sings in unison with you, as your soul soars to heavenly heights.

"Always give praise to the Father, the Son and the Holy Spirit. How Heaven rejoices with those who praise and adore Him unceasingly. So much grace comes to a soul who gives constant praise and thanksgiving for everything. My love is yours."

Jesus: "My people, do you ever wonder what it was like for Me in the days before going up to Jerusalem to begin My Passion and ultimate death? I had no true support other than My Mother who understood completely what must occur. It was her love and encouragement that allowed Me to wait, to continue one day, one step at a time the Path to Calvary. Being human, I was assailed by temptations to flee, to escape, to impatience, to despair.

"Flee to My Mother, dear ones. Escape into her Immaculate Heart. Bring your impatience and thoughts of discouragement to leave with her, as you hide from the hatred of the world within the safety of her Mantle. I tell you, this is the only behavior which brought Me the strength and courage to follow that Path, but more importantly, to wait for the actual day, decreed by My Father, for it to begin. Remember dear ones, the outcome of prayer and obedience is holiness."

> *"Give thanks to the Lord who is good, whose love*
> *endures forever! Let that be the prayer of the Lord's*
> *redeemed, those redeemed from the hand of the foe."*
> [Psalm 107:1-2]

GRATITUDE

Blessed Mother: "*My little ones, when you have finished each task of your day, and before you go on to the next one, please stop and give thanks to the Father for that task and all that He allows you to do for Him. Gratitude is a necessary ingredient on our way to holiness. Appreciation of God's gifts will help us to realize more and more what a privilege it is to be allowed to serve God and His people. It makes us aware of the different gifts the Father has given to us, and how He is now allowing us to use them! All of the things we do, children, are a result of God's gifts to us. He allows us to then serve Him and each other by using these same gifts. All that we have has been given us by God and, without His presence at every moment, we would have nothing and be nothing!*

> '*Praised be the Father Who gifts His children.*
> *Praise to Him Who continues to call His people to re-*
> *turn to Him for more gifts.*
> *Praise to Him Who longs to gift us with Himself for*
> *eternity.*
> *Praise to Him Who allows me to come to all of you,*
> *and speak to you, and pray with you.*
> *Praise Him, children, with every breath.*

Seek to please Him in all you do.
Remain hidden with me, and you will learn quickly that
TO LOVE IS ALL!

"The very act by which you were created by Love Itself calls you to love as you are loved. The very Love, which
sustains and nourishes you, calls you to sustain and love
everyone you meet with the same fairness and equality and
acceptance that you have experienced from God. That same
gift of love is free, My dear ones, free to be enjoyed and
developed and passed along to fill the world with beauty
and carefree laughter and peace and safety. The destruc-
tive forces which exist in your world today cannot be allowed to continue. The Father has decreed that there has
been enough suffering by all; and the cleansing power of
His Love, His Divine Son Jesus, will rid the world of everything that is not of love, not of life. Pray, children, and
praise the Father."

Do Whatever Love Requires

Chapter Four
Eucharist

MEDITATION FROM SAINT MARGARET MARY

"My dear brothers and sisters in His Sacred and Merciful Heart, I, Margaret Mary, come to all of you today as your hearts have requested and as His Sacred Heart has led me to speak to you.

"To love as He loves, (He Who is in His Real Presence to everyone there in the Tabernacle, in the Blessed Sacrament of the Eucharist) is what all souls, all hearts should desire and strive for. He has taken on a smallness in His humility to be hidden there in the Blessed Sacrament, in that little Host you receive in Communion, and in the Host you see in the Monstrance. He does this because of His undying love for you His beloved children.

"The more times you come to adore Him in His Sacred Presence, whether in front of Him in the Blessed Sacrament or through Perpetual Eucharistic Adoration, or in the receiving of Him in Holy Communion, you will begin to realize the gift He has given to all of mankind... the precious gift of His Real Presence among men.

"How happy the heart, the soul who believes in His Real Presence in the Eucharist. Generations upon generations who have believed in His Sacred Heart, in His Real Presence, have been given many graces to continue to open their hearts in trust even more to Him. He calls all to devotion to His Sacred Heart and, as you open your hearts to receive Him, He grants to your heart greater understanding of what His Heart is giving and what His Heart wishes in return from you.

"It so pleases me as one of His instruments to now see more come to know Him and have devotion to His Most Divine, lovable Sacred Heart. It gives all of Heaven a delight beyond words to see more come to Him in their nothingness and in humility, trusting that He is indeed with you and among you and will be until the end of time.

"Oh what preparation He, in His Sacred Heart, is giving to all of you for what is in store for each of you in Heaven one day. How precious your hearts and souls become to Him as you abandon completely yourselves to Him, to His Heart, taking your littleness, your nothingness, your weakness, your sorrows and giving them all to Him for His good pleasure, to use to heal not only you children but a world so in need of Him and of His Healing Heart.

"You then are given His strength and courage and much perseverance, obedience and patience which will be flooding into your hearts from Him. He then sees what you are lacking, as you give more to Him, as you allow Him to venture into your heart from His Heart; as you listen and begin to know in the silence of your heart, to recognize Him when He knocks, when He seeks you out.

"He especially gives you much strength as you accept and continue to carry the crosses He bestows on you, giving you much enlightenment, help and courage. The heart then knows that He is there to help in the carrying of these crosses and that He would do anything to help you. Then your heart will accept anything which would give pleasure to the Divine Heart Who wishes to be with each heart. His Heart wishes to have your heart for His very own. Oh what joy you will experience in acknowledging Him, adoring Him, receiving Him in the Eucharist, telling Him by this of your love which you give back to Him, Who is Love.

"That, children of the world, is how you learn to be one with Him, with the Most Holy Trinity. Always seek Him out. Always accept what He desires of you, willingly and with a complete desire on your part of pleasing Him and Him alone and then letting Him do with you as He Wills.

"What joy! What Heaven you will experience now as a prelude to what lies ahead for each of you in His Heart. This should be your goal; the salvation of your soul, other souls, pleasing Him in everything, accepting Him in love, in all ways.

"Please Him by pleasing His Mother, the Most Blessed Virgin Mary. She is your greatest ally in coming to know His Heart through Her Heart. I, your friend, Margaret Mary, who is now here for you in Heaven, wish all of you to be here as Saints one day with us. I wish you to be able to be in His total Presence for all Eternity. I shall be praying for you and with you for this. Call on me often to help you overcome any obstacles which may be impeding your progress of coming into His Most Sacred and Merciful Heart. My love is here for you now and always.

"Thank and praise Him for allowing His Saints to speak with you. We know how you feel and what you should strive for, because we have been there. Call on us often. Call on your Angels always for their help and, most importantly, call on the Holy Spirit for much needed guidance and direction, along with His Spouse, the ever blessed Holy Mary, Mother of God, a mother to all of us, is our Queen and Mediatrix of all His graces which He gives to Her in abundance to distribute to His children, Her children who ask."

Note: St. Margaret Mary had this revelation from Jesus, from His Sacred Heart, when first given this devotion to Him. He made her read in His Heart the following words: "My love reigns in suffering. It triumphs in humility and It rejoices in unity."

*"How lovely your dwelling O Lord of hosts! My
soul yearns and pines for the courts of the Lord.
My heart and flesh cry out for the living God. As
the sparrow finds a home and the swallow a nest to
settle her young, my home is by your altars, Lord
of hosts my King and my God."*
[Psalm 84:2-4]

REAL PRESENCE & ADORATION

Blessed Mother: *"Children of My Immaculate Heart, Jesus
is present in His Body, Blood, Soul and Divinity at every
Mass and when you receive Him* **in the state of grace***, nothing makes Him happier. It makes the Father happy as you
become one with Jesus in the Eucharist. Too often there
are those that come to receive His Precious Body and Blood
and are not in the state of grace. This offends and hurts
Him so much. When you receive Him with a mortal sin on
your soul, you condemn yourself. You are saying No to
Him. Give Him your lives and your wills. Repent now, as
this is truly a time of grace for all humanity.*

*"My priest sons, as well as my children, are to teach
the Gospel message. Please My little ones, bring more
people to the knowledge of My Son through the Sacrament
of His Divine Presence on the Altar at the Consecration
when He transforms the host and the wine into His Precious Body and Blood, His Real Presence with you. His
Presence in the Blessed Sacrament is much avoided by
people in the West. My priests need to tell the value of His
Real Presence to my children and then give them the ex-*

ample of their own presence with them in prayer in His Eucharistic Presence.

"Dearest ones of My Heart, My Jesus needs your prayers and your adoration. He especially needs that time alone with each of you when you visit Him in the Blessed Sacrament. When you open your hearts to Him, He can do much for you. I invite more to come before My Son in the Blessed Sacrament for private prayer with me, opening hearts and minds and giving all to Him through Me, the Immaculate Virgin Mother.

"Our plan is to have Perpetual Adoration flourish in all Our Churches in the world. When it does, many will come, grace will abound and there will be many conversions. As you reach out to the young, teach them the great value of devotion to Him in the Eucharist (in Adoration of Him, their God, in the Blessed Sacrament). Then you will experience a rise in vocations. Many will return to the Faith because of Perpetual Adoration. Eucharistic Adoration is the life blood for souls. It is He, your God, reaching out to you, His creatures, in His love and mercy, giving Himself to you in His Real Presence before you. It is most important all my children spend as much time as possible (according to their state in life) with Him.

*"In prayer with me, in front of the Blessed Sacrament, so many graces and blessings are given to those who come. **This is no longer an option!** Pray to the Holy Spirit to open up the time when you feel there is no time to spend with Us to be in complete union with Our Hearts. So much can be accomplished by this small effort on your part, dearest children. Tell others the importance of this as an exten-*

sion of the Holy Mass, the Sacrifice that takes place on His Altars all over the world. If my beloved Pope can take the time for adoration, how can you not?

"Pray many prayers to the Holy Spirit. Invoke His grace, His gifts on you. This way each will feel the urgency to become an Apostle of Mercy, an Apostle of Prayer and Apostles of the Most Holy Eucharist. You then will be filled with the desire to spend more time with Us in adoration.

"Here He can feed you, give you grace needed to go out as His Apostles to tell of the immediate need for all to come to Him in this Blessed Sacrament where He waits for each with a hunger and a love that far surpasses anything you can imagine.

"Children, my love is always with you as is My Heart when you come to Him to praise, to thank, to love, to just be here for the love He has to give and to give Him the love He wants in return. When you spend this time, what tremendous blessings not only for you, but for the many souls who will benefit from this, as you unite and give each visit to His Sacred Heart through My Immaculate Heart for the honor and glory of God. When you are in adoration, you are uniting with Jesus and myself on Calvary and then all the Father can say is YES to what is asked of Him in His Son's Name and Will and in His Precious Blood. What a treasure you then will have for souls, as all are brought before the throne of the Most High. If you could but know how love and mercy flow out to souls as grace, as merits, as a crown to souls, you would all come often to Him, praising and thanking Him, giving all to Him especially your wills. This is the greatest gift you can give back to Him, as then love becomes com-

plete. He can, as you can, then truly say your hearts are one.

"I am the MOTHER OF THE EUCHARIST. I am His Holy Mother. I am always at His side next to each Tabernacle, each Monstrance, adoring and pleading for my children who ignore Him. I am pleading for the Father to forgive those who blaspheme. Through His Precious Blood, through Perpetual Adoration, many miracles happen and will continue to happen. Adoration of Him and believing in His Real Presence is what will bring my children, His children back to Him and to His Church. Many conversions will then be seen. Your Churches will overflow. If only you would come and acknowledge Him as King of Kings, Lord of Lords, your God and Savior and only means of salvation."

Jesus: "My children, come to Me in the Blessed Sacrament to be refreshed, to seek shelter, to know how to find love and then to give it to others. This pleases Me. Come to Me in the Eucharist, as I cannot dwell any closer than when I am with you through your receiving My Body, Blood, Soul and Divinity in Communion. You are then filled by the 'Spring of Life' and have that 'Blessed Manna' that only I can give to nourish the soul and the body.

"Dear children of My Eucharistic Heart, when one feels the hunger to come to Me, to see Me, to be with Me, to adore and love Me in the Blessed Sacrament, you begin to understand how much I have to give, how far reaching My love, My mercy is and always has been and always will be. As I look at you and you look at Me, oh the currents of mercy and love, the energy, the fire that consumes your souls as you let Me completely wrap Myself in you, in your heart, uniting your heart with Mine. There then is a complete trust on the part of man for their God through Me in this Blessed Sacrament.

"Angels surround the Tabernacle. They surround the Monstrance of Exposition and sing out their alleluias in praise and thanksgiving for this union of hearts, man's heart to God's Heart. Graces come doubly to a soul who believes I am present even though not seen. You then see Me with your heart. My Presence in the Host is Real, is Divine, is Human, for I AM! I AM and always will be here for you who come to be refreshed. This is My gift of love to you. Your peace, joy and love come from being in My Presence. I am alive and smile at you, taking you into the deepest recesses of My Heart. This I do with all who come to adore and love Me. Listen for My beckoning in the silence of that place that is Mine in your heart, where My Mother and I take comfort. Remain in stillness, in peace, so you will never miss an opportunity of Our being with you and conversing with you.

"Love Me always and in all ways, not only when you need something. I know your hearts. I know your needs. I answer your heart prayers, for you are Mine. All are Mine who are consecrated to Me through My Mother's Immaculate Heart. My little ones, you My chosen, you know who you are, for you are My vessels. You are My instruments. You will be used and filled in different ways for the coming of the Kingdom. You are to help Me in the task of saving souls. You are to come now before Me, every day for at least one hour, a 'holy hour'. A visit to Me in the Blessed Sacrament means to be refreshed, to be renewed, to receive My peace and the graces necessary to carry on your vital missions according to the plan of the Heavenly Father.

"I am your Jesus of Mercy Who speaks to you. Praised be My Father Who gifts you with every sort of good thing. Praised be His Divine Plan for the salvation of His children. Thank and praise Him at every moment for His gracious goodness on your behalf. Give Him all the love in your heart and think of the Most Blessed Trinity every time you think! You are seeking unity with My Will. Please seek the help of My Mother more often.

"To sit in My Presence is your greatest gift as a member of My Body! It is the Will of My Father that all His creatures adore Me and love Me by sharing these silent hours with Me. I am indeed a prisoner for love of My children. If you would only realize that this is not a chore, but a blessing, a time for healing and strengthening.

"Please continue to come to Me and make My Presence your home. I will be with you after all vestiges of My Presence are removed by the enemies of My Church. It is important for you to keep telling this to My people and to encourage them not to feel abandoned. They must not believe that I have left them alone, even though they do not see the Blessed Sacrament, nor have the sacrifice of the Mass celebrated. This will be a time for building and practicing faith in all My words to them."

*"O God, you are my God — for You I long! For You
my body yearns; for You my soul thirsts, Like a land
parched, lifeless, and without water. So I look to You
in the sanctuary to see Your power and glory. For
Your love is better than life; my lips offer You
worship! I will bless You as long as I live; I will lift
up my hands, calling on Your Name."*

[Psalm 63:2-5]

SACRED HEART

Jesus: "My dear ones, your Lord is here waiting for you always. Do not ever feel alone or lonely, My sweet ones, but run to Me Who always awaits your company and your love. Know, My children, that I am always with you, and *you have only to pause to notice My Presence*. In the coming months, it will be necessary for you to do this often to strengthen yourself. My Presence will be like food for your weary, hungry heart. It will be a balm for your soul and for the wounded ones you will bring to Me. If you are constantly living in My Presence, you cannot feel lonely or unloved.

"You are continually being showered with Our love and special graces. This time of waiting is a very blessed time in which you are practicing obedience to My Father's Will for you. There is nothing greater for you to do, My dear ones, to prepare for the future. Please, be at peace. Continue to wait in quiet acceptance. Offer each breath, each prayer, each action and word to My Sacred Heart for the honor and glory of God, My Father.

There will never be anything you can do which would help to heal and strengthen you like the power of just being with Me and visiting in front of My Blessed Sacrament. Focus on Me and My Mother, and all the horrible suffering of Our dear ones throughout the world. Notice the difference constantly between your life and theirs, and allow their pain and suffering to be the impetus for your industry on their behalf. Notice how quickly the time is running its course. That time and those days, those opportunities, can <u>never</u> be recovered, My children, and so efforts need to be redoubled, the focus greater than any in your life so far. No prayer or effort is too small on behalf of My loved ones who will remain, feeling so devastated and alone.

"Watch and pray. Listen and lament the fate of all those who will not watch and pray and listen. Peace and joy are about to disappear from the land. You must find the joy and hope in your store of treasures that you have hidden where moisture can-not creep in, nor moth destroy. Wherever your treasure is, your heart and Mine will be.

"My littlest ones, when you come to adore Me, breathe deeply of the sanctity here before you in My Sacred Eucharist, this holy Sacrament of My Presence, this beloved gift of My Father to all of you. Soak up, bathe in the Sacrament of My Love for you. See the longing in My eyes and feel the tenderness of My Heart. No where else is this available to My people who wish to be close to Me in the oneness of My Blessed Trinity. Please give proper thanks and praise to Him Who loves and blesses you to this degree.

"My dear ones, I beg you again, never look back even to yesterday. Once a sin is confessed, it is gone forever. Take the residue, the knowledge you have learned, to strengthen your own resolve to persevere in times of great danger and even greater temptation. Encourage and strengthen each other. Be the direct channel of grace between My Heart and all those who need the strength and peace that is so necessary now in order to persevere in fortitude. Little ones, be firm in My love for you. Each day that you spend in quiet and prayerful recollection is a bountiful storing of ammunition with which to fight the enemy.

When you are weary, seek rest in My Sacred Heart. When you are lonely, seek comfort in My arms. When you feel empty, take courage and be filled by My Presence in the Blessed Sacrament. When all looks bleak and overwhelming, come to My Mother and Me, and We will refresh you with Our words for your understanding.

"The understanding of each human on earth is limited by many things. Especially, the mind is confined by what it can perceive. To understand a mystery more fully, one needs to enter into it more fully. Therefore, the *more you are united to Me*, the *more fully you have surrendered yourself to Me*, the *more you will know who I am* and understand how things happen in our relationship.

"It is My greatest desire to be more intimately united to all of you, to have you melt into My Being with all of who you are and all you will become. The mystery of our *oneness can only be explained once it is experienced* and, even then, it is a *matter of degrees and increases*. The growth into becoming Me, united to My Heart, more like Me, is a matter of death, death to yourself and your heart's desires and your personhood. Your whole person will become more divinized, more Christlike, the more you spend time in My Presence, commune with Me, love Me and be loved by Me.

"To study My actions and words while I lived, even those I have spoken to you all of this time, will give you a certain knowledge, examples to follow in order to be My follower! But *to become one with Me is only accomplished by the two of us being alone in order to absorb each other's being, presence, essence: The true knowledge of My Selfhood perceived by gazing, listening, contemplating and reflecting.* This is what you are constantly invited to, My children, to absorb the essence of Me in the closest proximity of the Eucharist, in the company of My Sacred Heart displayed in My Blessed Sacrament. There is no other way to gain the union of our wills that I offer to you. Come, and rest in My arms for the rest of eternity. There is nothing that you will miss, nothing that you will be avoiding, nothing that you cannot do without. The victory, the outcome of your endeavors, depends upon the degree of unity, of oneness that we share. Take advantage of all of Me. Take My strength and gifts to use as your own. Take the power of the Trinity which is possible to those who dwell within Our Oneness. Surrender more to Me. Allow your Jesus to be your all in all. Pray for My Father's Will to be done and then thank and praise Him for it."

Blessed Mother: *"Soon the time will come when there will no longer be an opportunity to visit My Jesus in His Churches, or seek peace before Him in the Sacrament of the Altar. Man will no longer be able to hear my voice or the voice of My Son. Then will the hearts of all who love me be saddened and heavy. They must be filled with faith and hope in their God Who has not abandoned them, but remains hidden in order to purify His people and fulfill the Scriptures. This will be a time of great suffering, for the feeling of abandonment will be very present in the world. Hearts will not sing, nor will the worship of the One, True God be allowed. Hearts will look about in terror for a safe place to go. Many will be the tragedies that will occur. I, their Mother, wish to warn them and help them and protect them.*

Woe to those who walk in darkness, for they will weep and wail and gnash their teeth when My Son returns with His Angels on the clouds of glory. Then the light will shine even more brightly for all to see their terrible deeds and witness their fiery descent into the deepest realm of hell, there to suffer torments forever, begging for even one drop of water to touch their tongues and ease their torment. This is not a torture to wish upon anyone. So, children, you must continue to pray constantly. Continue to seek My Son."

> *"In all wisdom and insight, He has made known to us the mystery of His Will in accord with His favor that He set forth in Him as a plan for the fullness of times, to sum up all things in Christ, in heaven and on the earth."*
> [Ephesians 1:8-10]

PRESENT MOMENT

Jesus: "Think of nothing else save being with Me, walking in My love and sharing My thoughts and feelings. When a soul is in love, nothing is too good for, or too great a task to perform for, its beloved. Any suffering or hardship is considered no trial at all when it is performed at the request of the One Who is loved. The time spent serving the Beloved is a mere second on the clock of Eternal Love. The joy at serving the Master overcomes all fatigue, all thoughts of other plans, and in order to please her Master, the soul will wait in silent patience just to be available for the least desire of her Beloved.

"What is necessary for you and what is pleasing to Me is what will be. Do not attempt to seek anything other than My Will. If you do not mention specifics, you will not be burdened with anxiety or questioning. Peace is the result of total trust that all which happens is according to My Plan for you. Please, spend each day doing your work and accepting what comes as My Will and desire for you that day.

"Stay in the present moment in a deeper awareness of My Presence and be comforted by a knowledge of My love. The heart grows impatient when it is not at rest. The heart cannot be at rest when it is consumed with questioning and requests. Be content with what is and know that this contentment is the only way you can be aware of My Presence and love for you. Seek Me in peace and docility. Be content with My desires for your future and each thing that this will mean for you. All have the opportunity to be renewed by My hand if they will only ask My forgiveness and pledge to Me their sorrow and eagerness to repent.

"It is a humble act to beg. It is a saving act to beg forgiveness for one's sins and confess them to Me. Praise the Father and thank Him for His gifts and, above all, His Divine Will in your life. Whatever We request of you is the result of His Will for your life. If you would live that Will totally, you will not ask questions regarding the future, but wait in humble obedience for all to occur. Docility is a difficult virtue. Only with the help of the Virgin Mother will you be able to live in this way.

"Praise and gratitude to the Father for His gifts opens the way for more of His gifts! The Father's Will is always being fulfilled in each person and the events of each life. He knows exactly what each one needs to allow a full return to Him in sorrow and repentance. So do not question, but wait and see, love and serve all who come to you and trust that the Father's Will is being accomplished.

"Please My children, be at peace. Continue to wait in quiet acceptance. Offer each breath, each prayer, each action and word to My Sacred Heart for the honor and glory of God, My Father. The knowledge that you are living in obedience to His Will gives you a peace and security like nothing else could. A backbone of steel is developed by allowing Our words to build up in you a core of strength. Only a peaceful, trusting waiting in My Presence will equip you for the future. Again, it is not for you to do, but just to be. An instrument is picked up by the Master when it is needed, and laid down again after the fact!"

> *"Then the angel said to her, "Do not be afraid,*
> *Mary, for you have found favor with God. Behold,*
> *you will conceive in your womb and bear a son,*
> *and you shall name him Jesus." "On the third day*
> *there was a wedding in Cana in Galilee, and the*
> *mother of Jesus was there."*
> [Luke 1:30-31 & John 2:1]

MARY, MOTHER OF THE EUCHARIST

Blessed Mother: *"Dearest ones of My Immaculate Heart, when I am honored and venerated as Our Lady of Guadalupe, your Mother of Mercy, I am the woman of Light, the "Woman Clothed With The Sun". Yes, I am as a 'River of Light' from which His Light passes to all of my children. It pleases me to be honored and venerated as Our Lady of Guadalupe and under all titles which have been bestowed upon me. You do well to also honor me under the title found on the "Miraculous Medal", as I am THE IMMACULATE CONCEPTION, the Immaculate one of God and the Mediatrix between My Son Jesus and man.*

"When you bring all to me, there is a direct channel to the Father through the Son and through My Spouse, the Holy Spirit. When difficulties arise, dear children, call me, call on the Holy Spirit and there will be fountains, rivers of grace poured into your hearts and souls to help you overcome the obstacles that the evil one is putting there. The adversary cannot survive in a soul, a heart that belongs to me, but he can threaten and make you doubt. Come and pray with me every day for all your needs and for peace. I am the Queen of Peace and come to show my

children the way to peace through Him, through His Divine Mercy and His Divine Will.

"In all my humility and obedience, God the Father accepts my pleas, my prayers as given to His Son and His Holy Spirit. Do not hesitate to follow me. Take my hand. Come with me into the sanctuary of my Immaculate Heart for refuge and comfort. I will show you the peace and glory that awaits you in His Most Divine, Merciful and Loving Sacred Heart. There is to be for all time the connection between man and God. It is I, the Virgin Mother of the Son. I am the Immaculate One who intercedes for all my children.

"Come and feast on goodness and mercy at the banquet of His Kingdom. All are invited, but so few come. Continue on the road that leads to Our Hearts and to doing His Will through me, His Mother. I am Queen of Heaven and Earth and I will conquer the evil one. This is happening now. Come join my army and come to the front where you will see the glorious Reign of your King. Pray many Rosaries and Chaplets of Mercy, giving all to me for souls. I know where this should be used for the honor and glory of the Father, the salvation of souls and conversion of hearts. Always praise and thank the Triune God for everything.

"Precious ones, give all to Me. Do all with me, in me through me, and for me, asking always for my spirit and disposition and renouncing your spirit, the spirit of the world. Come with your joys, sorrows, sadness, your every thought. When you call on me, on Jesus (His Holy Name) to take the spirit of the world from you, your life will take on a new dimension of holiness as you have replaced your spirit, (the spirit of the world), with Us. Your prayers, your genu-

ine concerns (for family and those whom you have come to know through grace given to you, through me, through My Son) are now to be left with me. They will be tucked in my Immaculate Heart. When you ask for this, it will be granted. All will receive a secure refuge in My Heart, sheltered from the storm that comes. Continue to hold all in your prayers, especially asking for His mercy to touch their hearts, so they will realize what it is that will be asked of them and how their God needs them to come willingly to Him.

"THE FATHER, through His Son and My Son, has given me graces to dispense as I will and to whom I will. Those who have been consecrated to me will always have a safe harbor in my heart and will be in communion with Jesus and in His Sacred Heart and Will. As you live your total consecration to Jesus through me every day, you then do all in Him, through Him, with Him, and for Him. There should never be a doubt in your minds about this. When your faith is weak, pray to the Holy Spirit to strengthen this faith and then trust, live in hope and have faith."

Jesus: "My dear ones, only those who come to know My Mother will truly come to know Me. It is My wish that you remain near to her, learning from her and allowing her to bring you to My Sacred Heart. Please spend more time with Me in silence in front of My Blessed Sacrament. There I wish for you to pour out your heart and all the shame and questions and hurts that are gathered there. I wish for you to abandon yourself to Me more completely so that I can work My Will in you. You are precious in My sight, My dear ones, and I love you so very much."

"When Jesus saw his mother and the disciple there whom he loved, he said to his mother, 'Woman behold your son.' "
[John 19:26]

MOTHER AND QUEEN

"I AM YOUR MOTHER, My beloved children. I want to hold all my children, to love them, to counsel them, to let you know how I feel. I want to direct you in what you should be doing. I am always here for you. I am your gift from God the Father. Jesus is your Gift. The Holy Spirit is Gift and has many gifts to bestow on hearts and souls. Please do not refuse these gifts from the Father for no one can survive without them. Much grace and mercy abound and are bestowed on all who accept these gifts from your beloved Jesus through me. Take all these gifts given you, listen to the Holy Spirit for guidance on how to use these gifts and then use them wisely.

"Abandon all to Jesus. You must have complete trust, love and faith. Come to the foot of the Cross where many mysteries will unfold. Follow me. Follow Jesus. Your hearts

89

are what We want. This is the key. When you give all to Us you will see wonderful and miraculous happenings. You are needed by the Father. You are all His instruments in His plan which cannot be stopped. Listen to The Holy Spirit's directions and my promptings for there is much to do for souls. We want all souls. Will you help Us?

"Pray. Pray. Pray always, for conversions, for vocations, for sinners, for peace (in hearts and in the world), pray for your priests, bishops and Our son the Pope, pray for each other and yourselves, pray for my intentions. You will be overwhelmed at the joy this will give Jesus as He shows His Mercy to all. Help us NOW by your prayers, your adoration of Him, your Masses, Communions, your works, your trust and your love.

"I will never stop interceding at the foot of the Cross for you and yours whom you have given me. Trust me for I am your Mother. Reach out and take my hand more often. I am never far from you. My Angels are always with you. No evil can penetrate through your wall of prayer and fasting. With a clean, purified heart come to me, so I can give your heart as a great treasure to My Son with love.

"I am the Queen of all Virtues, Mother of all. I am here to help you who want to grow in holiness and virtue. Pray from the heart more for the virtues you need. Ask the Holy Spirit to guide you in this and to help you overcome your faults. I am with you to help in this and in the renewal of the Church. I am with you to help in the renewal of the family, but I cannot do this alone. I need your help, my loved ones. Pray and give me your prayers, so we can defeat the adversary who is trying to stop my plan for this renewal in the Church, in families and in all your hearts."

"And Mary said: "My soul proclaims the greatness
of the Lord; my spirit rejoices in God my savior.
For he has looked upon his handmaid's lowliness;
behold, from now on will all ages call me blessed.
The mighty one has done great things for me, and
holy is his name."

[Luke 1:46-49]

JOY AND SPLENDOR

Jesus: "Dear children of My Sacred Heart, remember how Mary, My most beloved Mother, from her earliest childhood pondered things in her heart. Learn from her. She has much to give you from Me, from the Father and the Holy Spirit. She is closely aligned with Our Spirit and it is as We were one. She is the Queen of Heaven and earth and your hearts. The Holy Trinity bestowed this honor and grace on her from the beginning of time. We are one with her heart. Where she is, We are. Never doubt this. In her you have the master teacher of all, especially in the virtues and Our virtues. Listen to her as she leads you to Me and to your eternal happiness and peace.

"Stay within the boundaries of My Sacred and Merciful Heart, always coming under the protection and love of Mary's Immaculate Heart and under Her Mantle of Protection. She is grace. She is love. She is all you need as a guiding light to Me with Her Spouse, the Holy Spirit. Do not let go of her hand or be out of her reach and sight. When you do things with Mary, in Mary and through Mary, you are doing them with Me and in so doing, you are glorifying the Father by all that you think, say, and do in My Name. Praise the Father always, giving Him your hearts.

"When one thanks Me for Mary, it is as it should be and as all should do. She is a treasure, a gift of undying value which has been given to all My children. She is all beauty. She is the splendor of the Angels. She is Queen of Heaven and Earth. She is the Jewel in the crown which lights up the Heavens and the earth for all to bask in its beauty. She is Mother. She is joy beyond comparison.

"She is yours and She is Mine for all to come and enjoy her tenderness and her mercy. Come often to her and honor her, as you then crown her with your love and prayers. All Heaven rejoices when they see her being honored. She leads many souls to Me, including those who are in Purgatory.

"When you adore and praise Me through My Mother, you please Me very much. *Those who do not honor and love her cannot love Me*. She is the gate into My Heart. She holds the key. Tell everyone to bring all to My Sacred and Merciful Heart through My Mother's Immaculate Heart. No one is ever refused when this is done. When they see her, they see Me. I want all to know the intensity of My love, the way I love each of you through My Sacred Heart. This can be done through prayer and bringing all to Me through Mary. This then is complete consecration.

"I gave My Mother to all My children from the Cross. You are now all her children as well. Do you realize the precious gift which was given you? She brings all her children to Me, to the Father always. She pleads for you and with you, enabling you to see the Holy Spirit working in your lives. She prays that you realize We know your needs for your lives and that your ultimate goal should be the salvation of your souls and to be united with Us for all Eternity in Heaven.

"Continue with Mary your Mother and your Angels and Saints to pray for souls, especially those who are brought to My Cross and who are lukewarm, not knowing Who I Am. Pray that they accept the abundance of grace I wish to give each through My Mercy and Love and by WAY OF MY PASSION, DEATH AND RESURRECTION. I love each so very much and would certainly die again, a death even a thousand times more insidious if it were possible, for just one soul to be saved. That is how much I love. My Love is unfathomable and cannot be understood by the human mind and heart. One must just accept in faith and trust that this love, this mercy, will never change. I am unchangeable because I AM, and always will be. I LOVE AND AM LOVE."

Do Whatever Love Requires

Chapter Five
Divine Will & Love of God

MEDITATION FROM SAINT
CATHERINE OF SIENA

"I am Catherine from Siena, who speaks to you. Dear little servants of Our Lord Jesus Christ, you have become instruments of our words so that all may be further converted and prepared for the great Day of the Lord. It is a cause for much excitement for all of us in Heaven, as we watch you strive to be ready to receive Him and live now in His Will. In my time on earth, I was so ignorant and unprepared for the gifts of God. The Lord in His great tenderness and patience spoke to my heart also, telling me truths that were given as gifts for all His children. It was necessary for me to have every aid and assistance, so ignorant was I.

"Please to not be alarmed, people of the world, at what our great God and Father is working in your lives. He acts out of the greatest love for you and wishes only to bring you back to His knee. There He will further caress and bless and heal you in order to bring you into His Kingdom at the appointed time. It is so necessary for all of God's creation to be cleansed of the power and influence of the evil one. So great is his deception that you are not aware of how contrary to the Will of the Father is the life each one of you is now living.

"All self control and discipline is a way of being, a personal mode of behavior that is totally absent from your life style. Even the prayers and penances are done without the degree of love for the Creator that is necessary to give Him the proper honor and praise.

"Little ones of the earth, please listen to all that Jesus Christ and Our great Virgin Mother are saying to you in these times. Please, please dear ones, answer from your hearts with all your energy and sincerity the requests of the holy Mother to all of you. It is necessary that a serious amount of intervention on the part of Our Father be experienced by all the people of the earth. No one is exempt from the need for a large amount of cleansing and purifying.

"Nothing the world has ever known will compare to this gift of seeing your souls and life reviewed before the eyes of your heart. Nothing can overwhelm you if you realize that your loving Father acts to bring you into a conscious realization of what each must do to change and be saved. In my day, doing penance was a privilege!

"When I walked among the children of God and served the Lord Our God as best I could, it was a dreadful time of sin and turning away from God. In this present day, there is nothing in the past that can compare with the depth of evil and depravity now existing.

"Please dear children of God, listen to the words of Our Mother and her Son, your Savior. Turn back now and receive the graces and great love of your Creator. It is His Will that you are saved and come to Him now through the Hearts of Jesus and Mary. If you do this, you will know eternal bliss and happiness, peace and serenity, secure in the Eternal Kingdom.

"We wait for you and pray in union with all your loved ones here. I am Catherine who bids you be of good cheer and joy and hope for a future bright with the light and love of the Triune God. All of Heaven is praying. Be strong and persevere."

> *"The covenant which I made with you, you must not*
> *forget; you must not venerate other gods. But the*
> *Lord your God you must venerate."*
> [2 Kings 17:38-39]

THE JOURNEY

Blessed Mother: *"Dear children of My Immaculate Heart, when all things were created, God fashioned everything in His Divine Will. As the Creator lacks nothing, He wanted His creation to want for nothing, especially His most perfect creation, man whom He made in His Image and Likeness. Accordingly, man and woman lived in complete, absolute harmony, peace, love, joy, knowing how to please the Creator by a oneness in His Divine Will. This harmony of being in His Will was broken because of the sin of pride and disobedience through the cunning temptation of the fallen Angel Lucifer. Instead of the constant 'yes' God required of man through the gift of free will, man chose no longer to be submissive to the Will of the Creator.*

"Man, like Satan, said 'no' that first time to God. It was then the Father, in His sadness closed the gates of Paradise to man for a time. Because of Original Sin, Satan has been able to convince many over the centuries that man can be as good as God. By masterful deception, he has been able to turn man from God to a world of sin by man's saying "NO, I will not serve" as he had centuries ago. Because of His unfathomable and merciful love, God promised to give man another chance. He promised a redemption and a re-entry into the Kingdom through

His only begotten Son Who is, was and always will be One with Him.

"Man then had to deal with living on his own after being turned away from Paradise. Nevertheless, the God of the Universe never left man nor abandoned him to his own wiles. God was always there hoping for the best in man to shine and to image Him once again. He gave humankind guidelines by which to live as He wished, promising to send a Messiah, a Savior Who would open the gates of Heaven to them once again.

"Dear ones, as you continue your path to holiness, sanctity and to complete, absolute submission to His Will, it will not always be an easy way, but one that will hold for you, who decide to travel it, a glorious rainbow at the end of the journey leading to His Divine Will. Divine Will is LOVE. It is absolute. It is mercy beyond human comprehension. It is possible to be submissive to His Will and in harmony with Him, the Creator.

"You will see, as you travel this journey, how it will lead to Him, to His Will and away from what the world would have you believe as being the ultimate joy, happiness and love. Through my Immaculate Heart, you will be learning to be submissive to His Will and how it is possible to find the Kingdom on earth and a closeness to the Creator as was always planned. As generations advanced, the Father in His mercy and love kept His promise sending His only Son, Jesus, Who became a man through the working of the Holy Spirit. My Jesus was crucified and died for all His children so they once more could gain entrance into the Divine Will and Heaven. They could now start liv-

ing in the Kingdom while still on earth, if willing to give Him absolute charge over their lives, their bodies, hearts, souls and wills for His pleasure, to model once again His Perfect Image and Likeness.

"Jesus through His Death, Resurrection and Ascension was victor over death (sin) once and for all time. Jesus showed you that to die to sin is to say 'yes' to Him, to the Father. When you give Him an unconditional YES, you have then said you will be willing to suffer as he suffered, to love as He loves, to take up your cross and follow Him on that rugged path leading to holiness, sanctity and His Divine Will. What joy awaits those souls who decide for this path of suffering, of letting God be God, to control them in all things.

"No matter how much you will suffer, how or what you give up because of Him, deferring to His Will will bring much joy and peace. You will then know you are one with the Creator, as was always planned. You will look beyond the present circumstance and see Paradise. You will see Heaven with the eyes of the heart and the eyes of the soul. You will know that the reward awaiting far outweighs anything that can come or befall you in any way while on this journey to the Eternal Life of happiness.

"My children, please try to realize that being in the state of sanctifying grace is an important element to accomplish His Will in your life. He cannot deal with a soul who rejects Him by sin and that is exactly what happens when you are not in the state of grace.

NOTE: Grace is the free and undeserved help that God gives us to respond to His call to become children of

God, partakers of the Divine nature and of Eternal life. Sanctifying grace is an habitual gift that perfects the souls itself to enable it to live with God, to act by His love. It is the gratuitous gift of His Life that God makes to us; it is infused by the Holy Spirit into the soul to heal it of sin and to sanctify it. Taken from **Catholic Catechism**; Pages 483 & 484 / Sec. 1996, 1999 & 2000.

"God is the One Who never changes. His relationship with you is always the same: love, mercy and trust which are unfathomable to the human mind and heart. As your relationship grows, you begin to see Him as the only Good you will ever need. When you get to know Him, your love and mercy toward Him grows and it grows for others and yourself at the same miraculous time. All this is done through prayer which is the communication, the conversation you have with Us. He will then give much grace, through the Holy Spirit, when one asks it of Him. Now listen, My dearest ones, sit before Him in the silence of heart to heart prayer, letting Him, His Words absorb your beings and then trust in faith what He wishes of you and from you. Then follow Him!"

> *"So that the genuineness of your faith, more*
> *precious than gold that is perishable even though*
> *tested by fire, may prove to be for praise, glory, and*
> *honor at the revelation of Jesus Christ."*
> [1 Peter 1:7]

Jesus: "Dear ones of My Sacred and Merciful Heart, *continue to always praise, thank and adore Me.* Your prayers then touch My Heart and will not go unanswered. If you strive and wish to be in My Will, *go to Mary* the Immaculate One, as she guides all who wish to submit to Me in all things. *Completely abandon all for Me,* keeping focused on Me and within My Heart through My precious jewel, My Mother's Immaculate Heart. *Ask My Mother* each day how to please her as there is nothing she does that does not please Us, the Most Blessed and Divine Holy Trinity.

"When you love another unselfishly, thinking of the other above yourself and wanting to please only the other above your feelings, paying no heed to what others may be saying to discourage you, you will then be making inroads into My Heart, into My very Being and into becoming another Me. When you *live in Our Will in trust,* you will be able to endure much suffering as I did for souls, for the salvation of many and for yourselves.

"You will never question what is being asked of you but will *do all in love,* peace and in the simple faith of a child whose eyes are focused on the One it adores, admires, loves and Whom it trusts completely. *You will trust in blind obedience* all I give you. You will *do all I ask* because your will no longer exists, only Mine. The Triune

God will live completely and in total harmony with you, with your thoughts, your feelings, with your heart and with your soul. Do you see where this can be difficult for most? To give of oneself is not of the human nature because of Original Sin. As one learns to *know Me,* to *lean on Me,* to *love Me* above all else including your very self, you will begin to *believe in faith* with the wisdom of that simple, humble childlike trust in Me and Me alone.

"When you start to *depend on Me, calling on My Divine Mercy,* living all My Mother and I have taught through the ages, asking for the *grace* and the *virtues* needed to overcome self and your faults, barriers will begin to disappear, changes will take place and you will start to see with your heart and soul - ME - and will want nothing then but to please Me, nothing but to be with Me in Our Divine Will. Only with much prayer, fasting and sacrificing and the following of Me, living in My mercy, showing My mercy to others, to yourself and to Me your God, can you find yourself then wanting to be in that Light of Divine Will as the Father had always planned it to be.

"Dearest ones, come, come all of you who want only Me and see how wonderful it is to be with Me in The Divine Will. Pray with Mary, your mother, and St. Joseph often, always asking them to take charge of your very person, your hearts, your wills and to show you how to submit and to abandon completely to My Will. You will find many stumbling blocks along this way, many obstacles, as the adversary hates a soul who is fashioned in Divine Will, as he hates the one who is doing and living My Divine Mercy. Do not falter, if this is the rugged path you wish and have chosen to take, as the reward is the greatest gift you will ever receive. Come then, when you feel you are ready to enclose yourselves in The Divine Will of the Most Holy Trinity.

"Children, listen and strive to be in complete and total submission to My Will. It is the only hope and solace you will have in the future months ahead of you. Practice always your total Consecration to Me through Mary the Immaculate One. Live My Divine Mercy in all you do, think and say and never cease praying and staying close to the shelter of Our Hearts. Your Angels and Saints will be there to help, as all Saints have traveled this same rough road to Divine Will. Come and you will see the joy at the end, the joy of being totally one with Us and in Us, living only as was always planned, as it was in Paradise and is in Heaven. I love all My children so much."

*"Now this is eternal life, that they should know You,
the only true God, and the One You sent, Jesus
Christ. I glorify You on earth by accomplishing the
work You gave me to do."*
[John 17:3-4]

GOD THE FATHER

GOD, THE FATHER: "My children, if you draw near the Heart of My Son, Jesus, and know Him through His Sacred Heart, you then know My thoughts. Always stay in that close relationship with Jesus, My Son, My dear people, and you will know all there is to know about Me. My Heart is pure Spirit, as is My Son's. Therefore, We have the Third Person of Our Trinity, Our Holy Spirit. We are One. We are One God, and all works to the good of nature and My universe when My creation recognizes Me as God the Creator, God of Love and Mercy. If you know the Son and the Mother and you know Our Holy Spirit, you know Me. There is no way, when One dwells in a soul, that the Others are not there as well. I am your Father. I am God and Creator of all mankind, of all Creation. YAHWEH. Love Me as I love you. Then once more all will be well with My world.

"There are things to come which I had always hoped would not, since Adam's fall, since Lucifer disobeyed with his pride, this pride and disobedience of two of My beloved that closed Heaven for a time to My beloved creature, man, and sentenced those angels to an Eternity without Me. I had hoped with My gift, your treasure of free will, you would have conformed and united this gift to My Will as I had meant it to be, but as you are free to do and to choose (as Lucifer and Adam and Eve were), some have not chosen to follow Me.

"I then sent My Son to show the way, to save all from eternal darkness, a darkness brought on by yourselves because of pride and your disobedience to Me. My Son was correct. Those who will not love as We love and who will not serve as We serve, will be lost. As a good Father, I must punish those of you who are rebellious, who have not taken My love and mercy seriously. I do not want this, but there is no other choice.

"My little loved ones, you must not fear (those of you who are in Our Will) for you are being protected from the danger of losing your souls. Some of you may not survive this tribulation that must come, but there is a reason for this too. Some will be old, some will be weak, some too young to help themselves, to help each other. Those of you who will survive will live in peace and love and will strive for Heaven on earth. You will see My Son and My Mary, the flower and jewel of My Kingdom. You will walk with My Saints. Some will even see their loved ones. There will be many to help those of you (the remnant who will be left) put My world back the way it was always meant to be. It will be a glorious time.

"Pray for My Son's Second Coming. My Hand is about to fall heavily on some, lighter on others. Know I only do this out of love and mercy for all of you, My creatures. You were always meant to live with Me, to see Me, to love as I love. Now I must re-create all anew. For those who have faith and love in their hearts, love and peace will reign again very soon. Your hearts will belong to Me, your Creator, the only God of all. Follow My Son to Me!"

"Awake, O sleeper, and arise from the dead,
and Christ will give you light."
[Ephesians 5:14]

THE FATHER'S LOVE

GOD, THE FATHER: "My dear ones, be filled with My peace and a great love for Me. I love you! There is nothing greater than love, which can unite us. Even suffering, if done with joy and love and surrender, is the unity that is accomplished only when two people love each other. That is only possible when My grace is received by people who put all of My needs, all of My desires before their own. The more you surrender your will to Mine, the more you will have My grace and peace. I am a God of Mercy Who wishes only the best for My people. I have called to them since the beginning of their creation, yet the lure of the senses clouds the reality of My beauty and goodness. The excitement of the moment befuddles the mind and causes My children to lose the Way. These, children, are problems of faith. These are the results of sin and turning away from Me. Do not think that it has ever been different. The pain in the lives of My people has always been so great because of the resistance offered by them to My simplicity, My good judgment on their behalf.

"The ability of My people to resist Me is given greater strength by the presence of evil in their lives. Those who indulge each whim, each desire, will never be in My peace until their own needs are not first, their own desires do not consume them. Their own fury rages and destroys that peace which I long to give them. The ability to dwell in thankfulness for the moment, no matter what the occasion, will allow My children to overcome their struggle and gain the freedom necessary to allow My will more completely.

"Do not be fooled by your own understanding of Me. Seek only the gifts of understanding and wisdom of My Spirit. Sit before Me in silence and ask for these gifts, if you would seek to truly know Who I Am. Allow My Spirit to direct you more completely, more fully. Practice this, My people, for it is a knowledge you need, if you are to learn to love Me and not your own concepts of Me.

"When you are truly humble before Me and bring a repentant heart for Me to heal, I cannot resist you, nor deny your requests. Oh My dear people, how I long to reveal Myself more fully to you, if you will only allow it. You must come in simplicity and seek My Kingdom in simplicity, and wait in simplicity, and be grateful at every moment for what has been and will be. I promise you My love forever!

"I need for you to desire to love and know Me and then to serve Me, all in a greater way. I am waiting for you to seek Me, My dear children, in total simplicity and openness. Please, My dearest ones, desire Me as I desire you. Seek Me as I am seeking you. Pour yourselves out in praise and love and gratitude, as I pour Myself out for you. Let us begin now to walk arm in arm in peace and simplicity so that My joy may be yours and your joy may be complete. Anyone who wishes to serve Me must be willing to wait in peace for Me to act in their lives. My Spirit will let you know when these times of action are to occur. The benevolence of a loving Father always acts for the very best interests of His child. Always, live in the faith and trust that I am performing good for My world, for My people. I am your Lord and your God Who is and was and will always be."

> *"For we are the temple of the living God; as God*
> *said: I will live with them and move among them,*
> *and I will be their God and they shall be my people."*
> [2 Corinthians 6:16]

SURRENDER

Jesus: "Please, surrender more to the peace and silence of My company, the ardor of My Heart, the burden of My tasks, My Will for you. Breathe deeply, dear ones, the odor of My Sanctity, the sweetness of My Presence, the air of mystery which surrounds this Sacred Place, this Blessed Sacrament of Mine. In your future lies total abandonment of yourself to the Will of My Father.

"Ponder again the greatness of My Father's love and gifts and mercy for you. It is the way to holiness. It is the means to the perseverance you desire. The ability to serve faithfully does not happen, is not given all at once. It is built, develops day by day.

"In looking back to remember God's gifts, you will be filled with more gratitude which, in turn, will feed the desire to continue to serve Him in fidelity. Gratitude is the key to the Heart of the Father. The morning of each day sees the world renewed for whatever comes. Let each morning be a new beginning of your own preparation for the Will of My Father. Thank Him first, dear children of My Heart, and then listen for His whisperings of love. Please, seek to build up now the secret well of grace and strength deep within yourself, so that you might dip into this refreshing treasure trove and be renewed and strengthened. There will always be chaos around those who serve Me, but as long as you stay united to My Heart and wrapped in My Mother's Mantle of love and protection, you will be filled with peace. Those who come will be filled with My peace also when they choose to open themselves to My Spirit. This has always been so!

"These opportunities will seem even more special because of the terrible conditions that will exist everywhere. The contrast between the chaos in the world and the quiet and peace of My Presence will, itself, draw people to Me through all of My chosen ones who seek to bring My lost children back to Us.

"Be the supple flowers blowing in the breeze of Our Spirit. Allow yourselves to be sent in whatever direction is willed by My Father, and you will soon feel more comfortable living in this free and unencumbered way. The light of the world will soon shine only from within the hearts of My faithful ones. Allow yourselves to be emptied more and more, dear ones, and be filled with My Presence that My Light may shine upon all.

"The outcome of prayer and obedience is holiness. The fruits of virtue are born by the spirit of those who dwell in the Garden of My Father's Will. Here, all is peaceful and each action is fruitful. Here, the effects of your response are completely united to My Heart and the heart of My Mother, and are totally able to affect the lives of all Our children. They are in such need of My mercy, My dear ones. You see more clearly how much I need you as vehicles of this mercy. Without it, My children will be lost forever.

"Do not attempt to seek anything other than My Will. If you do not mention specifics, you will not be burdened with anxiety or questioning. Peace is the result of total trust that all which happens is according to My Plan for you. The heart grows impatient when it is not at rest. The heart cannot be at rest when it is consumed with questioning and requests. Seek Me, dear ones, in peace and docility. Be content with My desires for your future and each thing that this will mean for you.

"Forsake all others, My people. This does not mean you do not love them or will not serve them. You love and serve Me when you do it for them. This means that no other desires fill your heart than to be united to Me and My desires for you. My Sacred Heart will pour forth all of its love and mercy and power through you when you are that close to It. We must be inseparable from now on, so that I may work My Will, the Father's Will, in you and through you. And when the Father gazes upon Me with love, He will see and be gazing upon you with the same love.

"Please tell all My dear ones not to worry about anything. All will be taken care of according to My Father's Will for each of them. It is time to act with honor and courage on behalf of their Lord and to trust that I will care for you, each of you, My chosen ones. Doing Our Will, My dear ones, is the greatest act of mercy you could perform for the world.

"Everybody wins! Most especially, you are being merciful to My Father in Heaven when you allow Him to work through you His Will for His people. Without an instrument of free will to use for His purposes, the Father chooses to remain helpless. Without your willingness to obey all He asks of you, the Father could not continue His Plan of Salvation for all of creation. He has chosen to work through His people as instruments of Divine grace and mercy and love.

"Unless someone says 'yes' to His invitation, nothing can be accomplished. It is so true that you were created through no choice of your own, but you will not be saved without specific choices on your part. This is the mystery of God's love. Everything you could ever need is completely at your disposal, but you must choose to love, to forgive, to have mercy.

"My sweet ones, My own Heart can heal you when our hearts are placed close together! There is no other way to experience peace and gratitude. The cup of My love spills over from My Heart onto yours and bathes you in contentment and a serene love. These are results which last forever. Whatever happens, please just say, 'Amen' and 'Hosanna' and continue in peace to live out each event in your life with perfect trust. You save yourself so much grief and anxiety by refusing to speculate on events and the times of their fulfillment. A CONCERT PIANIST MUST PRACTICE MANY YEARS IN ORDER TO BE PREPARED, My people."

> *"What if God, wishing to show His wrath and make known His power, has endured with much patience the vessels of wrath made for destruction? This was to make known the riches of His glory to the vessels of mercy."*
> [Romans 9:22-23]

MERCY

Jesus: "My beloved children, read Isaiah, chapter 30. These are My people now who pay Me no heed as in the time of Isaiah. Help them, My little ones. Please pray with Me to the Father for the many who have strayed from My Sheepfold. Offer them insights into My love and mercy. Be My light as you shine, showing them Me by your living examples of trust, love and mercy. Mercy is being proclaimed not only through Myself, but through My Mother throughout the universe. It has been brought to you through many Saints and most recently through Blessed Faustina in your century. We are asking and inviting all of you to be Our prophets, Our apostles, Our disciples of mercy and love. All of you have been given many gifts and graces. Please use them to proclaim My mercy.

"My mercy knows no boundaries. Therefore, anything of good, any sort of gift, no matter how large and overwhelming, can be expected to be given to My people if you pray and ask Me for it. The times in which you live and the influence of the evil one can only be countered by My grace and mercy. If you believe in that mercy, it will be freely given to you and to all those for whom you ask it.

Pray that all will then accept the graces and mercy being offered to them. Work unceasingly for the conversion of sinners. Bring to Me the souls that are most difficult, most impossible to convert.

"My children, please remember I am Love, Mercy, Compassion and Gentleness. I am all a soul needs. Use Me as I want to give, and give, and then give some more. The cup of My mercy, My love, My Heart never runs dry. Drink from this Cup. This is where your thirst and hunger will be satisfied. This is where you will find peace.

"Offer every act, every prayer for them. Our holy and blessed Mother knows who they are. Bring them to Me through her heart, in her hands, please My dear ones. The knowledge My people seek is so often not necessary for them to have. If they will only believe in My Mother and trust her, she will accomplish their desires by bringing their petitions and needs to Me. Together, We take them to the Father Who will refuse Us nothing! The need for patience and trust and hope will enable all of the graces, saved for each person on earth, to be released and showered upon their loved ones.

"When all is done and you see the saving power of God come to aid His people, you will marvel at His justice and mercy. NOTHING YOU CAN IMAGINE CAN AP-PROACH THE REALITY OF MY FATHER'S LOVE FOR HIS PEOPLE! Therefore, My dear people, give the Father praise and your own love and gratitude. He is your Buckler and Shield, the Warrior Who will accompany His dear loved ones into battle. Ask to be healed according to My Will, and it will be done, dear ones. Seek and you shall find. Knock and We will open unto you. I am your Jesus Who loves you. Amen. Amen."

Blessed Mother: "*Dear children, the Father, like all good Fathers in His mercy and love, will need to punish, to chastise those of you who are rebellious, who refuse to acknowledge His Son, to acknowledge me and to acknowledge the Creator as God. You are not gods. Your material possessions are not god. Your TV's and other activities are not god. So many put so much first in their lives and then work God in where they feel it is convenient for them. No! Your priorities are confused. The world of the evil one has convinced you that you (and what you want) are the most important things. No, I say again. This is not the way it was ever meant to be. Your God is God. He made you in His Image and Likeness to love and serve Him as He does you. Then He gives you all else according to your needs and His Will. He knows what it is you should have and when. Do not strike at Him by not taking Him seriously as God. HE IS LORD. HE IS GOD. HE IS THE LOVING FATHER OF ALL. HE IS THE ALMIGHTY, MOST HOLY ONE!*"

*"Blessed be the God and Father of our Lord Jesus
Christ, Who has blessed us in Christ with every
spiritual blessings in the heavens, as He chose us in
Him, before the foundation of the world, to be holy
and without blemish before Him. In love He destined
us for adoption to Himself through Jesus Christ, in
accord with the favor of His Will, for the praise and
glory of His grace that He granted us in the beloved."*
[Ephesians 1:3-6]

THE DIVINE WILL

Jesus: "Please listen, My people. Your ability to change is
only a matter of openness to the gifts We wish to give you.
In the quiet of doing nothing, strength is built up. In the
quiet of listening, obedience is developed. In the quiet of
just being, love will flood your hearts because We have
the chance to love each other and be further united! In these
days, the graces are ten-fold because you are required to
wait on My Will for you and bow to My commands.

"The essence of loving Me and being united to My
Heart and Will is perceived and experienced by trusting
all I tell your heart and request of you. Take note of the
changes within yourselves and give thanks to the Father
for His many gifts to you. Without the gifts of Our Father,
sustained by My love and the intercession of My Mother,
you would be no better than the pagans who live in the
world, worshipping false gods!

"The Father's Will is always being fulfilled in each
person and the events of each life. He knows what each
one needs to allow a full return to Him in sorrow and re-

pentance. So do not question, but wait and see, My dear people. Love and serve all who come to you, and trust that the Father's Will is being accomplished. All of your chores are little match sticks building a mighty edifice of praise and love for Our Heavenly Father!"

"Do not attempt to seek anything other than My Will. If you do not mention specifics, you will not be burdened with anxiety or questioning. Peace is the result of total trust that all which happens is according to My Plan for you. The heart grows impatient when it is not at rest. The heart cannot be at rest when it is consumed with questioning and requests. Seek Me, dear ones, in peace and docility. Be content with My desires for your future and each thing that this will mean for you.

"Forsake all others, My People. This does not mean you do not love them or will not serve them. You love and serve Me when you do it for them. This means that no other desires fill your heart than to be united to Me and My desires for you. My Sacred Heart will pour forth all of its love and mercy and power through you when you are that close to It. We must be inseparable from now on, so that I may work My Will, the Father's Will, in you and through you. And when the Father gazes upon Me with love, He will see and be gazing upon you with the same love. Please tell all My dear ones not to worry about anything. All will be taken care of according to My Father's Will for each of them. It is time to act with honor and courage on behalf of your Lord and to trust that I will care for you, each of you. My chosen ones. Doing Our Will, My dear ones, is the greatest act of mercy you could perform for the world."

Chapter Six
Suffering & The Cross

MEDITATION FROM SAINT FRANCIS
AND SAINT ANTHONY

"Our Lord Jesus and the Queen of Heaven, our Mother, have asked me, Francis to speak to you, all Their children and all of you who I pray and intercede for at every minute of your day. Praying to be in Heaven is something all should strive for, should be preparing for at the very outset of your lives on earth. You will find, as we have who are now in our heavenly home, that your journey, your pilgrimage on earth is but a short distance to what you will spend in eternity with all of us.

"I would urge all who read these words of mine and those contained in this blessed booklet which Jesus and Mary have given you, to seriously put them into your hearts, asking the Holy Spirit to open your hearts so your minds will see and think with your heart, with Their Hearts.

"It took me some time when I was on my earthly journey to realize the fact that my focus was not always on what He wanted of me, what He planned for me, and what He willed for me. It took me the rest of my life searching for this light of His. At every turn I took when He called and when I said my unequivocal yes, I followed Him and what I felt He was asking of me.

"I carried my crosses in obedience, trust and love in each direction He bade me. There was much suffering in my life and there will be in yours, if you wish to truly follow Him. All suffering and crosses are not of the physical kind. Those of the soul are sometimes more trying and painful.

"For whatever He wishes of you, pray for the grace to say yes to Him at every turn and to never look back, to never give in to the evil wiles of Lucifer and to the temptations he will throw in your path. Keep your eyes on His cross which is THE CROSS, as so much understanding will come to you when you open more to Him, giving all of you, your hearts, souls, wills.

"Even in the light of rejection, ridicule, pain and suffering, humiliation and many trials, you will learn unconditional love. You will be following Him, living as He showed each of us by His own life while on earth, and now through many prophets to His children ... especially through His Mother. See Her and you see Him. You will see truth. You will see light. You will see the way to Him, to the life here He wishes for your preparation to the eternal life He wants for all of you in Heaven with Them.

"My close friend, Anthony, now wishes to speak with you ... I send you my love, prayers and support. Call on me. I am here to help each of you join us here in Heaven one day."

"My brothers and sisters in Christ Jesus and His Immaculate Mother Mary, I Anthony salute Them for this opportunity to praise our God for His goodness, mercy and love, for allowing me to talk with you. My life, as yours, was not always easy and in most cases very much the way of the cross.

"My dear friend Francis has said many things that affirm my feelings and thoughts. In addition I would like to urge all to continuously pray for conversion, for yourselves, for others. Without a conversion of heart you will not be able to accept anything of what our God wishes for you, for you will be too much imbedded in the world and of the world. Your need should be to be in His Spirit and with His Spirit. This is done by constant, vigilant prayer to Him for this grace to be able to hear His voice and for the grace to willingly change the areas of your lives that He will speak to you about.

"Without this you will not have a true conversion. You will be walking and being in the dark and not in the light, His Light. Call on me, my dear brothers and sisters. I am you brother Anthony in Heaven, who will help you, who will intercede for you for this grace, this precious jewel of conversion of heart, of change, of coming back into the arms of the One Who loves you with so much tenderness.

"To know this and to be in His care while on earth is what you will need to be living as He wills for you and preparing yourself for your permanent home here in Heaven with all of us for eternity. Oh what joy, peace and understanding will fill you when you completely abandon yourselves to change and come to Him wholly.

"My love is yours as are my prayers. Ask me for my intercession and help in all your needs. Go now and live in His peace, love and mercy always. I wait to greet each of you here in our home."

"But we hold this treasure in earthen vessels, that the surpassing power may be of God and not from us. We are afflicted in every way, but not constrained; perplexed, but not driven to despair; persecuted, but not abandoned; struck down, but not destroyed; always carrying about in the body the dying of Jesus, so that the life of Jesus may also be manifested in our body. For we who live are constantly being given up to death for the sake of Jesus, so that the life of Jesus may be manifested in our mortal flesh."
[2 Corinthians 4:7-11]

SUFFERING

Jesus: "Suffering, My children, is the vehicle by which My people become human. Their hard hearts are broken by certain events in their lives which cause great pain. This, in turn, causes them to stop and reflect in ways they never would otherwise. Pain breaks down defenses and postures, affected strengths and rationalizations. One cannot present a false face to the world when that face is crumpled with grief or pain. Pain is felt in the deepest recesses of your heart and soul. Nothing else will touch you at that depth. Joy is also felt deeply in your heart. This is only after pain and suffering have broken open the ground of experience in order to receive the joy!

"Pain and grief drop seeds of joy which ripen and burst into bloom only after they are watered by the tears of remorse and repentance. This process is the result of My Father's love for each of His children. Without pain, man would continue to pursue lust and greed, power and ego, idleness and sloth. The pride which exists in the hearts of mankind is the sign of Satan's continued presence. As long as one continues to live a life of competition, anger and bitterness, selfishness and impatience, Satan will have his way with that soul. It is not until that way is broken, and the pieces of a life reassembled by Myself through Our Holy Spirit, that a life begins to be lived according to the Creator's plan for it. Until then, the soul cannot find Me or My Way because it is drowning in illusion, blinded by the false promises of the world. One is healed only by being patterned after My Life. This must happen for everyone before they can attain the salvation for which I died.

"The vessel is broken and remolded many times, because the action of change is very difficult for human nature to accept. The Father, in His gracious goodness, allows the soul to war against Him, resist and even run away, all the while calling to it. The Father gathers the broken pieces once more and puts them together in a better fashion each time this process is repeated. Slowly, gradually, the finished works more and more resemble the Son, the image and likeness it was created to reflect.

"Gradually, there is less resistance, less tension from each vessel, and it is then marked with My wounds. The more a soul resembles Me and contains the marks of My life, My suffering and death, the more like Me it will become in every way. Wounds and disease are caused by a split, a distance between the spiritual self and the worldly self. As long as this distance remains, wholeness and holiness cannot exist within that soul. The soul resembles Satan when it is scarred by his marks and identification.

"Children resemble their parents, look like them and act like them. If the soul belongs to the evil one, it will contain evil, reflect evil, resemble him in action, word and spirit. The cunning of the father of lies will dwell in that soul. The success of the world's promises will belong to its endeavors.

"When you come near to Me on My Cross, you can see how much I loved you and still do. When you accept your own cross: your weakness, defects, ineptitude, incompleteness, pain and wounds, you can bring it to Me. I will press My wounds against yours to heal them. You need do nothing but spend time with Me, the time it takes to fill you with peace after you have been emptied of the noise and chaos that lives deep within you. Only in the silence of contemplating My Cross and your own, and offering them to Me in unity, will healing begin. Only by accepting each event the Father sends to you with obedience and, above all docility, will He be able to replace the lack of strength and discipline needed to be a child of God.

"My suffering and death was the result of My love for you. Your suffering and all the little deaths, (your crosses,) are the result of My love for you, also. They are the grinding stone which smoothes the rough places, the hard edges, the brittle areas, the bumps! My love for you also sustains you throughout your pain and suffering, just as My Father's love sustained Me. As you accept your life with its crosses, you will begin to discover the joy that can be yours in surrender.

"Surrender to the Will of the Father is the Gateway to Joy! It is the narrow path which leads to the heart of the Kingdom. With it comes peace and contentment and security like you have never imagined. These are all gifts which are experienced deep within the soul, and are the results of allowing My heavenly Father to lead you, to determine your life events according to what He knows is best for your soul to come most quickly to a state of perfection and unity with the Trinity."

> *"For to this you have been called, because Christ*
> *also suffered for you, leaving you an example that*
> *you should follow in His footsteps. 'He committed no*
> *sin, and no deceit was found in His mouth.' When*
> *He was insulted, He returned no insult; when He*
> *suffered, He did not threaten; instead, He handed*
> *Himself over to the One Who judges justly. He*
> *Himself bore our sins in His Body upon the cross, so*
> *that, free from sin, we might live for righteousness.*
> *By His wounds you have been healed."*
> [1 Peter 2:21-24]

THE CROSS

Jesus: "Dear ones of My Sacred and Merciful Heart, I still suffer, as on the Cross, for the many sins of those who do not believe, who are indifferent. Prayer will make up for the many sins committed, as will mortification and sacrifice. Carry your crosses united with Mine, and you will see how easy (though seemingly difficult) things will become. Know to offer all suffering in union with Mine, with My pain on the Cross and you will discover peace, joy and love. Follow My Cross, My Passion in your hearts often and you will know how to suffer as I did.

"There will come a time all of you, in some way or another, will suffer. Some will suffer more than others for the salvation of souls. Some will see the Father's plan unfold in their heart, in all hearts that will be open to Him. This can only be done in close union with Me and with Mary, your Mother.

"When you travel the hill to Calvary with Me, with My Mother and stand beneath the Cross with her, immerse yourselves totally in Me, in My Passion and crucify yourselves with Me on that Cross. Die to yourselves that I may live totally in you and you may experience not only My Death and Passion, but My Resurrection. Please come often to the Hill of Calvary with Mary.

"When My children bring Me those souls you pray for and to My Mother who stands beneath the Cross, she will enclose these souls in Her Immaculate Heart and under her mantle. You then have taken the first step for those you pray for. It is then up to them to take the next and final steps to come here to Me beneath the Cross and express their love, their repentance for all their sins. Pray they embrace My Cross, as they willingly give themselves to Me through Mary, the Immaculate One, here at the foot of the Cross. Some will not be able to do this as it will mean a change, even a drastic change. This giving is of their wills, their hearts, their souls, their very lives and what they possess in the world. Most do not realize how great is the reward of the Cross. If they look up into My Heart, into My Eyes, they would see Heaven. They would see what Eternity will hold for those who willingly give all to Me. This is the choice each must make. No one, not even I, can make this choice for them."

Blessed Mother: "*Children of My Immaculate Heart, take your nothingness, your imperfect person, your sinful souls and give them to me. I will offer them to Him from my hands and from My Immaculate Heart. Give me all you* *are to take to Him including your tears of remorse, of re-pentance, asking forgiveness for yourself and the world and making reparation to Him for the world.*

"Jesus is the Word Who was made Flesh, died for all and rose from the dead once and for all time, conquering evil and sin. You must now help in this redemptive act with me. Help bring more of my children to the Cross to show Him to them and then offer Him your crosses in union with His Cross. His Cross was the sign, and still is, of love for all of us. Each of your crosses offered to Him and in union with Him through Me, is your sign of love for Him. How pleased He is when this is done. All will realize that the path to Heaven with Us in Eternity is filled with suffering and sacrifices, but also filled with the joy of the crosses He allows each to carry. Crossing the threshold to the King-dom can happen for you while still on earth."

> *"And Mary kept all these things, reflecting*
> *on them in her heart."*
> *[Luke 2:19]*

JOURNEY TO THE CROSS

Blessed Mother: *"You are seeking a greater union with me and My Son. Please, continue in this fashion, for of such is the Kingdom of God. All of Heaven contemplates the beginning of My Son's Passion this night, and you will be more surely united to me if you walk this Way in my company.*

"Allow me to bring you to the foot of the Cross. Allow me to show you the depths of my love, as I followed my Jesus from a distance through the streets lined with shouting, jeering people whose only thoughts were to kill my Jesus. Allow the feelings to penetrate your heart, as you hear these sounds and terrible words. See what they are doing to Him Whom I love. See how they push and taunt Him. I long to run to Him and shield His bruised Body with my own. A mother would always try to do this for her child, but I must stay away and allow all of Scripture to be fulfilled.

"My Son, the Lamb, must be slain for the very people who are screaming for His death. They are intent on destroying the One Who has loved and served them, taught them and healed them, eaten with them and visited in their homes; Who only wished to bring them knowledge of the Father and His great love for them. Can you bear to watch this scene, child? Can you bear to see His Sacred Blood

poured out on the filthy streets to mingle with the dust and dirt of the crazed people yelling for My Beloved Son's death?

"My heart was always filled with great longing to be reunited with My Son, and this was a longing which gave me an energy and love to serve His friends who also missed Him so, and spoke of nothing other than His words and recounted stories of His time on earth with them. Each day new marvels would be recorded, as an awareness grew within them of all My Jesus had done for them.

"I was able to be comforted by the recounting of all these times in My Jesus' life with His beloved ones. It brought me comfort to hear the love and gratitude in their voices, and for a brief time He would live for each of us again! We lived for the day that each of us would be called to Heaven to be with Him, all the while learning together from His words that were remembered. This was the way our days passed, in love and longing, never quite recovering from the horror of those dreadful days when My Son, the Lamb, was crucified. Join me now, My child, as we walk the streets behind Him and watch Him suffer and die. I love you, My child, and thank you for wishing to accompany Me on this awful journey. It begins."

Jesus: "My people, do you ever wonder what it was like for Me in the days before going up to Jerusalem to begin My Passion and ultimate death? I had no true support other than My Mother who understood completely what must occur. It was her love and encouragement that allowed Me to wait, to continue one day, one step at a time the Path to

Calvary. Being human, I was assailed by temptations to flee, to escape, to impatience, to despair.

"Flee to My Mother, dear ones. Escape into her Immaculate Heart. Bring your impatience and thoughts of discouragement to leave with her, as you hide from the hatred of the world within the safety of her Mantle. I tell you, this is the only behavior which brought Me the strength and courage to follow that Path, but more importantly, to wait for the actual day, decreed by My Father, for it to begin.

"Walk with Me, children, carry My Cross with Me, fall with Me and rise to continue to the Hill of Shame. Come now and be lifted up with Me, hang on My Cross and die with Me in perfect union with My Will for you. You will be Mine forever, as We become more completely united. It is this I have created you for. It is now that the Father's Will for you will begin to be fulfilled in its entirety.

"It is only a matter of moments now before My Passion begins. Won't you join Me every step of the way, and find out how much I love you now and how much I loved you then. Become acutely aware of all I endured for you. Become one with Me for this brief period of time so that I can show you all the things you wish to know, so that I can give you a drink from My Cup, so that I can sign you with the sign of My suffering.

"Please pray together with Us for the Coming of the Kingdom. THE SALVATION OF THE ENTIRE WORLD IS IN THE HANDS OF THOSE WHO PRAY. Will there be enough interested in saving their brothers and sisters? It is the central thought of all Our prayer requests, My little ones. Please pray so much more! I am your Jesus of Mercy Who comes in love and peace to fill you with Myself. Prepare yourselves each moment of the day to be emptied more totally and filled more completely with grace and peace and strength."

Chapter Seven
Spiritual Preparedness

MEDITATION FROM SAINT TERESA OF AVILA

"My dear sisters and brothers in the Lord Jesus Christ, I bring you tidings of hope and joy. I am Teresa from the Carmel in Spain who speaks words of love and greeting to you. It is from a great gift of God, our loving and merciful Father, that I speak. It is important in these special times of crisis in the world that we are all praying at every moment for the people of the entire world. The time left for prayer and conversion is very short. The words of Scripture are handed down to us for all generations, and it was these words and the guidance of the Holy Spirit of God that brought me through very serious and trying times, as well.

"Please listen with all of your hearts to the voice of the Spirit Who comes as a tiny whisper in the heart. He comes like a whisper so that all of God's children will strain to hear His Will. It is this kind of listening and attention that trains us in obedience and prepares us to fight against our inclinations to laziness and self deception. Soon the Father is granting to the world the grace to see clearly all that troubles each one, all that leads an individual into particular kinds of sin. It is necessary now, My dear ones, to be fooled no longer by the lies of the Prince of Darkness who rules the world with the greatest deceptions of all the illusions of power and intellectual supremacy!

"If you were to see Hell and all the souls who suffer there, you would be immediately convinced of the need to come back now to God the Supreme Majesty while there is yet time. The place in Hell that was saved for me and then shown to me through the gracious gift of God was enough to stop me from a life of self deception. I received the clarity of mind to accept myself as I really was and the strength and good sense to return at once to all I had professed myself to be.

"My dear friends and family, please pray at every second of time that remains in this era. Prayer must remain simple. Prayer must be an outpouring of your hearts and thoughts and needs to the Triune Majesty and the glorious Virgin Mary. Please, dear children of the Father, know that all of Heaven prays for you at all times. Believe in the power of your prayers to help lead you closer to our Jesus Who is weeping for love of you who refrain from responding to His great love for each of you, His children. The Father weeps and calls you by name with great and tender love. He wishes to save your souls from Hell and bring you into His eternal Kingdom.

"Prayer, my beloved brothers and sisters, is the conversation of hearts, the communication of all the Communion of Saints. We in Heaven call out to all of you upon the earth. **Trust the words of Scripture, the power of your prayers and the mercy of our Savior.** Please ask us to pray with you in this great time of need. The light of Jesus shines as a beacon to all who are lost and don't know where to go. There is relief and comfort only in the Hearts of Jesus and His holiest of mothers, the Immaculate One.

"As you begin to recover from the effects of the great events of this century, please stay close to the entire Body of Christ. Count on them and each other to be praying for you, as you pray for them and the reparation of sins. All who wait and serve their families in Christ are blessed beyond your understanding. It is time to be involved in the work of salvation, co-redeeming your brothers and sisters throughout the entire world. Love them and hold all in your hearts and prayers. Soon, you will all be even nearer to the Hearts of Jesus and His Mother, as They walk among you on a cleansed and renewed earth.

"The blessings of the Triune God and holy Mary adorn your souls, as you read my words and as you continue to live out these final calls to action on behalf of all those who will come in such need. Prepare their paths with your prayers. Pass on the legacy of grace as the greatest inheritance all will take along, as they venture into a new era of peace and joy.

"Children of God, I Teresa from Avila in the company of Jesus and the holy Angels, the Mother of all and my fellow Saints, send the blessings of the Triune God to the world and to each of you. We hear your prayers and send ours to each of you. We hear your prayers and send ours in return for your return in splendor to the Kingdom on earth as it is in Heaven. Persevere, loved ones of Jesus, and be warmed and cheered by my words of great affection for all of you who read."

> *"I will remember the deeds of the Lord; yes, the*
> *wonders of old I will remember. I will recite all*
> *Your works; Your exploits I will tell. Your way, O*
> *God is holy; what god is as great as our God? You*
> *alone are the God Who did wonders; among the*
> *peoples You reveal Your might."*
> [Psalms 77: 12-15]

THE BATTLE

Jesus: "The justice of My Father looms over the earth like a giant hand waiting to fall. The justice of My Father is like a sickle that will thresh away the weeds and the wheat to be separated by the Harvester at the proper time. My Father is the Harvester, My people. He is standing by with His giant scythe ready to swing it over the earth. These times call for drastic measures in order to clear the earth for new plantings. The earth must be tilled and turned in order to renew it. The soil must be aerated for proper drainage. Each seedling will yield a rich abundance for the time of reaping. My children of promise will receive the fruits of this planting and be nourished for the time to come.

"You will see what I mean when it happens, children. You will understand everything, as it is lived out. Events of the greatest magnitude are about to change the face of the earth, and especially your country forever. Be vigilant every moment of your day. There are many people who love and serve My Mother and Me. We love you all beyond what any words could tell. The future is dependent on love, dearest ones. The present is sustained by love and the past is a reflection of the love My Father has given to His people. All is about to be purified until only love remains!

"So many of My people are confused, and this confusion will only grow. My dear ones, My Father desires to clear the hearts and minds of His children so that nothing but His Will can dominate. This idea of domination is one which requires total surrender on the part of His people. When a leader takes His soldiers into battle, they must be of one mind and heart, ready to fight at any moment. A spiritual battle is no different. All must be in a state of readiness to stop every activity and fight for the protection of the weak.

"Please, continue to fight to build up your own strength and obedience to lead those who wish to follow Me. At different times throughout the history of My people, it has been necessary to cleanse them and lead them to a new land, one that has been promised to them in order to begin anew. The land flowing with milk and honey has been described throughout Scripture. If ever there was a need for a new land, a new world cleansed of evil, it is now, My dear people.

"There is no one able to fight Satan and his cohorts without the strength of God, Our Heavenly Father. It is He Who has created all. It is to My Name that every knee must bend. It is a new beginning My people need in order to return to the understanding of Truth as it has always been revealed and accepted by Our chosen people. There are many phases of this Plan to be worked out and lived through. It is not a Plan that will fail, although that will seem to be the way it will go. I cannot tell you how difficult it will be to persevere in spite of appearances, in the midst of seeming defeat and certain doom. No one who fights a battle could have the strength to endure without a strong leader to guide them. MY FATHER, OUR SPIRIT AND I WILL BE WITH EACH OF YOU AT EVERY MOMENT. Yet, My little ones of this world will need leaders to encourage and convince them to persevere until the end. All of Us in Heaven and on earth must wait in humble obedience and readiness for the moment the Father chooses to act."

"My soul rests in God alone, from Whom comes my
salvation. God alone is my rock and my salvation, my
secure height; I shall not fall. Trust God at all times,
my people! Pour out your hearts to God our refuge."
[Psalms 62:2 & 7-9]

SAFETY

Jesus: "Be grateful for each event that has developed in your life that has been a means of teaching you more about yourself and exposing every weakness that needs defending. In a battle preparation, one needs to inspect the line of defense (the walls) in order to shore up any weak areas. These areas are present in all My people. You know that the quickest way to learn is to experience. When one falls back from the front lines, it is to shore up, to recover and recoup losses, to rearm, to rest and ready yourself to return to the renewed battle. This will always be necessary, as long as sin and the evil one is allowed to prey on Our people. It is why We have spoken so often and waited so long for each of you to be made ready, strong and prepared for the ultimate battle.

"The evil one is cunning and subtle. You cannot know his plans, but you can be ready to combat his evil ways. Know and deeply trust and believe that My strength and the help of My Mother will be enough to sustain each of you who holds out until My coming back into the world. A soldier never knows how a battle will play out, but brings preparedness and obedience to the battle and a willingness to fight alongside the Commander.

"The outcome of the battle is assured, but it will take many turns before ultimate victory. It will always be necessary to count on My strength, on the help of the Angels and Saints surrounding you, to carry you through any occasion. The events will seem overwhelming many times, and only trust in Our words will take you beyond apparent defeat. If you ever feel the need of more help and strength, or that you are in danger of being overwhelmed by people and events, you have only to stop and retreat into My Presence (always with you), to be renewed, My people. Whatever you need will always be available to you.

"I remind you, dear ones, that an instrument is a lowly, plain tool picked up by the Potter in order to work with the clay while it is soft and pliable. Many such tools are needed to help form and mold the many clay pots in the Master's shop! Great heat is applied to the lowly containers. They are fired for just the right amount of time to obtain the proper glaze each one needs. These vessels are ornaments at the table of the Master which serve to nourish those who are invited to the Banquet. My Father and I are preparing the greatest Banquet in the history of Our people. Many vessels are needed to hold the nourishment for Our people starving for the Bread of Life, the Water of Grace, the Meat of Truth.

"Feel the embrace of Our Spirit and His strength and gifts coursing through your veins. Know that you are never alone and will never be overcome or abandoned, even though you find yourself alone for the moment. Believe and be filled with courage and conviction about all that is about to unfold. The Plan of My Father will unfold, as always, according to the needs of the greatest numbers.

"It is with a great sense of My own excitement that I speak all of these words. It is with great love pouring from My Heart to yours and filling you with My peace, and every gift you will need for the future, that I enfold each of My dearest soldiers in an embrace of love and healing. Be filled with gratitude, My dear ones. Thank My Father with every breath, with every ounce of strength and awareness as the final preparedness before the battle. We will never leave you. We will never let you down. We will shower graces on those who come to listen so that hearts will be opened to Our Words and will be healed. As you wait in joy and hope for My triumphant return to the world, the Triumph of the Two Hearts and the fulfillment of all of Scripture, come and adore."

> *"Turn from evil and do good, that you may inhabit*
> *the land forever. For the LORD loves justice and does*
> *not abandon the faithful. The salvation of the just is*
> *from the LORD, their refuge in times of distress. The*
> *LORD helps and rescues them, rescues and saves them*
> *from the wicked, because in GOD they take refuge."*
>
> [Psalm 37:27-28, 39-40]

RESCUE

Jesus: "The battle being waged by Lucifer is the ultimate battle for souls. It is the true belief of his henchmen that they will be victorious in this attempt to win souls for the cause of the world. Power corrupts like nothing else. The lure of money is a blinding force, and mankind is unable to think in a rational way. When I say, 'darkness is descending upon your world,' I mean a darkening of the intellect, the reasoning powers of the mind, the ability of the soul to choose for good. Man is so steeped in corruption, he is unable to see truth, to make rational decisions, to see the difference between good and evil. If a person is spiritually blind, he cannot see the difference between choices and so, chooses what is most pleasing, most gratifying and stimulating to his senses. Lust is at the core of most of the choices of My people. It has completely defeated the ability they had been given to make decisions for a noble cause, for the good of another, for the common good.

My dear people, to live in community, at peace with the rest, is only possible for a soul guided by motives of love and mercy. It is for this reason that My beloved chosen ones will live in this fashion to protect themselves from the chaos of the world. Death and violence will exist everywhere. Only in a hidden environment, removed from the violence of the streets and the violence in men's hearts, will it be possible to live in union with My Mother and Me. We will be there with you, although even this fact will be partially obscured because of the amount of evil in the very atmosphere. Your faith and perseverance will be tested to the last ounce of your strength, My dear ones. You will fight to the very end and the last moment before My coming. From now on, everything will be more and more difficult, as Satan attempts to defeat you and the work you will do for Me.

"Please break open these words each day and nourish yourself with them. Just focus on Me in the present moment *as though no danger exists* for you. The armour of truth will be your greatest strength. The cunning and wiles of the enemy can never prevail against truth. The truth will set you free on every occasion, little ones. Take refuge in My Truth and be comforted by it when there is no other comfort to be found! Dearest ones, do you know what it is like to be God and have Our hands tied by Our own creatures? Your God suffers great frustration, My children, because so many deny My entrance into their hearts. We have so many gifts to share, and no one is interested enough to bother finding out what wonders are waiting for them. You will shortly see such wonders and prodigies performed for the millions who come back to My Father.

"For a very short period of time, a Golden Age will seem to have blossomed across the land. But subtle fiends hidden these many years will suddenly come into the open and announce their evil intentions. Gone suddenly will be the effects of Our grace and mercy for so many newly converted souls. And you will see *treachery in families* the likes of which never has been witnessed on earth.

"Yes, there will be destruction of the land soon. Everything will come to pass before you realize it, nothing will ever be the same again. Nothing will be as you now know it, will ever be that way again. Confess your sins immediately, My people, and every few days after that! Keep yourself in as pure a state, as sinless as possible, from this moment on. We are All at your side to help you. You will overcome every opposition for My Father's sake, for the sake of the world. Think only of caring for your own needs now, so that the needs of all Our poor needy children will be properly served. All who wait, rejoice! The Day of the Lord begins with the dawn. The vengeance of the Lord against all the powers of hell commences. You are about to witness unbelievable struggles and hardships. Be brave and strong in My love and protection."

"The Kingdom of God is not a matter of eating or drinking, but of justice, peace and the joy that is given by the Holy Spirit. Whoever serves Christ in this way pleases God and wins the esteem of men. Let us then, make it our aim to work for peace and to strengthen one another.

[Romans 14:17-19]

BE AT PEACE

Jesus: "My dear little ones, the Wisdom of the Father is perfect! He knows each one of His children completely and perfectly! Please trust and ask all those who listen to Our words to do the same. The Father loves you all as though you were already in Heaven with Him. Please, thank the Father for each struggle and rejection He allows you to experience. Please, recall what a privilege it is to unite your sufferings with Mine for the salvation of the world. Please, be at peace. You are learning everything you need to know to render you ready and alert for every trick of the evil one. Do not despair over struggles. Do not allow your peace and calm to be destroyed by anyone.

"My dearest ones, when events begin, you will wonder where the time has gone. The impatience you feel is part of the preparation of your will. This will build discipline like nothing else. Our words are wisdom and light! All waiting is a small problem in light of the greater good that will be an outcome. Preparation to serve Our people is a joy when offered for the glory of the Father. Remember the danger ahead and recall that you are preparing to fight the greatest battle in the history of the earth.

"Children of the world, unite and come back to your God. Seize the moment and run to Me. Be assured of forgiveness and mercy. This has always been My promise to you. It has never been so important to believe and act on this promise! Soon all mankind will see their souls and the dreadful state of their sinfulness. Soon the adversary will redouble his efforts to win you away from Me. In his hatred, he will leave no stone unturned. No effort will be too great on his part, as he attempts to lure you with the empty promises of the world.

"As you are emptied, more of My grace and love can flow through you. Have confidence in your Jesus! Trust your Mother and Me. Remain recollected and quiet in order to gain strength and renewed vigor. Come to Me, your Divine Physician, and I will heal your wounds and dry your tears.

"My Mother will care for you with all the tenderness in her heart and, together, We will prepare you to meet My Father as We present you to Him! Waiting and praying and wondering is a normal part of the preparation period for My people who will fight the battle with My Mother and Me. Know that the Angels and Saints are at your disposal. Call upon them at any time. They are praying for you constantly and will help in your time of need."

*"Have no love for the world, nor the things that the
world affords. If anyone loves the world, the
Father's love has no place in him, for nothing that
the world affords comes from the Father; and the
world with its seductions is passing away, but the
man who does God's Will endures forever."*

[1 John 2:15-17]

TIME IS SHORT

Blessed Mother: "*Dearest of My Immaculate Heart, please
listen. Time is short dear ones and this is not just a figure
of speech. It is a reality! There is soon to come much of
what has been foretold in Scripture to many of My children around the world. You must prepare by spiritually
focusing on the condition of your souls and the Second
Coming of Jesus. Through being spiritually prepared in
your whole being, you will then see the Reign of Our Hearts,
the Triumph of My Immaculate Heart with the Reign of the
Sacred Heart of My Son, Jesus.*

"*These are glorious times you live in, this time of preparation. To the unbeliever it may be a frightening time. Always be in readiness, for no one knows the hour of your
destiny when it will be the time of your fulfillment of God's
plan for you in this pilgrimage on earth. Pray to be in the
state of grace at all times. There must always be much
preparation of the heart before important feast days. Much
prayer and fasting is recommended. Perhaps a Novena
before, as well. This should be done individually or in community. I, your Mother, want to form many prayer commu-*

nities, so those in these communities will be able to with-stand all that is to come. Then they will be guiding lights to others, a beacon for those who are in need spiritually and sometimes physically.

"My Jesus as Christ the King must be prayed to, adored, honored and put in His rightful place in your homes, lives and families. Please pray for unity. The importance no longer lies in the reading, talking and searching for another message from Jesus or myself. Come now, as I have asked many times, to my Immaculate Heart. Come back to God through prayer. Prayer has not been first in the lives of His people, especially those in the West. There must be a change, a change in hearts. This is the 11th hour of grace, of mercy, and that is why it is imperative to increase prayer.

"I will outline again what I have been saying so many times, the spiritual to-do's. Please try to go to Mass and Communion daily; go to confession regularly, monthly or even weekly now. Keep your souls in the state of grace. Have Perpetual Adoration when and if possible. Pray your priests will see the value of being in the Real Presence of My Son, through adoration, where graces untold are given and where I am always. Vigils of prayer are most important.

"If you cannot come to Eucharistic Adoration, then come at least one hour a day before Him in the Blessed Sacrament in the Tabernacle. He wants to strengthen you through this gift of Himself so hearts, souls and bodies will be filled with grace, always ready and prepared for what the Father has planned for you. Pray the Rosary, meditate on all the mysteries every day and pray The Chap-

*let of Mercy for souls. Take your Consecrations to Jesus through me seriously, consecrating yourselves daily, and pray for peace. Live the Commandments and the Virtues. **You must live each day as if it were your last.***

"Have purity of heart to be able to see God in all you do and in all you meet. There must be love, My children. Without love there will never be unity and without unity you do not have God. The lessons are so simple: faith, trust, love, conversion, all through prayer, prayer that will bring peace and purity of heart, mind and soul."

Jesus: "Children of My Sacred Heart, if your hearts and souls are prepared for Me at all times and are in union with Me, you will know there will be no need to be anxious over anything, let alone your physical well being, as all will be taken care of according to My Will and what has been destined by the Father.

"Isaiah is a most important book in the Old Testament, as is Daniel and the Psalms, as to what to expect. Especially important for meditation is Isaiah chapters 12, 13, 32 and 42. Psalm 37 is most relevant to what I have to say to all of My children. Read these often for your consolation. Zecariah's Canticle in the book of Luke is profound. I wish you to ponder and pray these words. Your salvation is assured if you follow My ways, acknowledging Me as your Lord and God.

"I will remember My Holy Covenant that I make with you to save this errant people of the world, if they but listen to My final pleas and come to My mercy and love. Serve Me all the days of your lives and be holy in My sight. I am the Day Spring and My mercy is visiting My people to let them know of My love. Nowhere in the history of mankind have there been so many pleadings, warnings, teachings and so much patience with Our creatures.

"God has been good, kind and merciful because He is a loving Father. He has given you, through Me, every opportunity of seeing the errors of your ways, with the ability to come back to Him and into His Loving Heart. So many of Our children are blind, spiritually blind, and have not seen with the eyes of their hearts. You now have to be totally prepared spiritually for what the Father has planned for you and for His world. You will see many more natural cataclysms occur: earthquakes, unseasonable weather changes (that cannot be explained by man), wars, eruptions and disruptions of every kind and in every nation. When the sun darkens and the moon will no longer shine know that I, the Son of God, will then come.

"Dear ones, I need your hearts, your whole beings, your prayers, fasting, sacrifice and I need them NOW for yourselves and all souls. Do not worry or become anxious for what the future may hold. *Dwell in Me.* Today is what is important and not tomorrow. Your sanctity, your salvation and the salvation of the entire world is what is at stake. Be at peace and in My peace. My dearest children, please strengthen yourselves through much prayer and then more prayer. PLEASE TRUST IN ME! There will be dark days ahead, yes, but the light that will shine through this will be blinding. This light will purify the world. There is nothing to fear, My little ones, if your souls are prepared and ready to meet Me. There will only be untold happiness and joy in Eternity with Us.

"Trust and believe that all is going to be purified and that there will be a NEW DAY. This will be a day in which love will flourish as it once did in the hearts of man. Everyone will be at peace as it was intended from the beginning of time. Please listen to the spirit of truth, only. It is now time to stop doing other things that take you away from Me. Listen. Live. Act on what We are telling you for your personal spiritual preparedness. You will then be a light for those who will need you and will seek you out in their needs.

"All are in the final process of purification and are to listen always and most attentively to the Holy Spirit Who, with Mary the Immaculate One, will be instructing and guiding each of you. There is no room for guile, for ego, for jealousy, resentments, anger and pride. These things belong to Satan. All must have Mary's humility, gentleness, joy, hope, faith, unconditional love, complete trust and abandonment to Me. You will then know My Wisdom, and much will be revealed to your hearts, as they will no longer be your hearts but Mine. We will then be as one, think as one, love as one, trust as one, pray, praise, thank, adore as one, the Almighty One - the Father.

"Dear children, be spiritually and physically prepared! That is why you are to be with Me in complete harmony. Those who continue to be busy all the time doing many things not of Me, who question My authority, are negative and seldom cheerful, will not be able to be properly prepared and will not be able to accept the grace and mercy I am offering to all. You must not, now, be busy about anything other than what My Mother and I have requested of you, bringing your soul and other souls to Me, helping Us in the harvest of souls in this time of mercy and through My mercy. What is mercy other than love, compassion, understanding, trust, charity, humility and obedience? Mercy is everything. Mercy is all the virtues and living them in My Perfect Will!

"No one is to give in to the evil one's deception through those who will try to lure you away from Me. If what you are doing is not leading to the salvation of your soul and the souls of others, beware. Stop and listen to your hearts. You must learn to live My mercy and be in My Will, forsaking all for Me letting go of self, taking up your cross every day and carrying it with Me, to a complete spiritual union between My Heart and yours. This is preparing yourself in the right direction for anything the Father has planned for you.

"I plead with you to continue spreading My mercy, My Father's mercy and to live it in your lives every day. Continue with Cenacles of Prayer. Please increase your prayer groups. Reach out to the corners of each of your states to make sure prayer is foremost. The Mass, is the primary prayer with Holy Communion.

"More need to see My joy, mercy and love in you and through you. My little ones, do not make grand plans for yourselves or others now, as there is only time left for My plans and those alone which I give each of you on a daily basis. This then will be a time for rejoicing. Man will then realize a happiness he has never had before **and I will once more be your only God** and true friend. Remember, I AM THE WAY, THE TRUTH, THE LIFE AND LIGHT. These words the world cannot do without."

"Finally, draw your strength from the Lord and from His mighty power. Put on the armor of God so that you may be able to stand firm against the tactics of the devil. For our struggle is not with flesh and blood, but with the principalities, with the powers, with the world rulers of this present darkness, with the evil spirits in the heavens. Therefore, put on the armor of God, that you may be able to resist on the evil day and, having done everything, to hold your ground."
[Ephesians 6:10-13]

PRELUDE TO THE KINGDOM

Jesus: "My dear people, soon a rumble will be heard across the land which will tear it in two. Soon cries of anguish will fill the air, and all who are willing must come to the aid of their brothers. Mayhem will prevail. There will be no safety in the streets, as people fight and loot and further destroy each other in fear and panic. Rally the forces around you into a team of people ready to minister to those who come, who survive this time. Encourage all to reach out to all in need with all you have. The food and supplies will not last long and will give way to conditions of famine. An extremely difficult time is ahead of everyone. Not only will there be chaos and bloodshed, but this nation will be crippled by one disaster after another. The powers of your country will be defeated by the overwhelming destruction and turn to other nations for help. It will be at this time that the enemies of freedom will come in and take over the control of your government. It will be then that the forces of evil will gain a foothold on the people and will force them into submission. This will be so subtle at first, as to deceive all who receive help. It will seem like the answer to economic woes and physical destruction.

"During these times, My people, My faithful ones will band together so as to lend strength and courage and aid to each other. This will also set up the time when you will be living apart from the rest of the country, growing your own food, living in virtual hiding from the powers that will overwhelm the land. In the days to come, drought and famine will deplete stores and decimate families.

"The government which controls your country will force men into labor, and women and children into detention areas as a means of controlling the people. Events will also come to pass that will *shepherd My faithful ones and keep you safe for further events.*

"In the meantime, dearest ones, spread My Mercy to all who will receive it. Be My beacon, My trumpet, My song which calls all to the truth of My Father. From now on, plans for battle will escalate and break over the people like a series of bombardments, explosions that will rock the land and split the firmament. The darkness which has developed is beyond description. You know nothing of this kind of evil and hatred, My dearest ones. Stay close to Love and prepare to suffer for Love's sake. Holiness is only achieved through suffering the Way, the Path to Holiness! Please, act always with the understanding that all of time is short, and there is none to waste on a delay in people's response to a Merciful God Who calls to them to come back in repentance to know, love and answer His call to them to become His heirs forever in His Kingdom.

"At the present time, leaders of the world are in full agreement about all that is playing out for the rest of you to see. Great deception marks each public event. Diabolical scheming is present behind the dubious events being presented by the media throughout the world. There is no honesty left at any level of government, as plots and lies are present everywhere. In the meantime, innocent people continue to suffer and die. My Church does nothing to help matters on the scale on which it should be working. My Church around the globe is the focal point of all wars and destruction, despite news to the contrary. It is this deception which allows enemies to continue to persecute those who follow Me.

"My Mother's enemies are everywhere, and know the great power she has been given against Satan. That is why they continue to downplay her role in My Church and will not cooperate with her requests throughout the world. It is a sad time to see, My people. It is a reason by itself to cleanse the world. But they shall see evil defeated and all of their plans brought to ashes.

"Dearest ones, it is hard to believe that so much hatred exists. When all is completed, it will be because the hatred of My people will have been spent. They will be emptied of venom and a desire to do evil, and destroyed. They will be exhausted by their own futile attempts to destroy My Father's world and control His people.

"THE REIGN OF GOD IS ABOUT TO BECOME A REALITY UPON THIS EARTH. Every promise, every word of Scripture will be fulfilled up to My Coming. Think of it! A new time will begin, and a renewed Church will grow and rise out of the ashes. What better place than out of the chaos of the hatred in men's hearts? What better argument for a new creation, a new world, than the need for renewed beauty in hearts and in the world. Do you not see how death upon the earth is needed before new life can begin? It is the law of the grain of wheat; the law of change and growth. It is the way it has always happened, My people.

"Please, tell My children that evil and ugliness can no longer be accepted and tolerated. The justice of My Father for those who love Him, and cry out for vengeance upon those who murder and rape and pillage, must begin now. The outrage is beyond words. The lack of respect and dignity has turned humans into creatures which resemble animals. It is a wonder My Father has put up with their behavior for this long. The deeds done in darkness are beyond description, and a merciful God must now come to the aid of His poor suffering children. No longer can they be objects of the whims of creatures bent on pleasure and greed. No more will He allow His innocent ones to suffer the sins of those who should be caring for them, cherishing their bodies and souls and thanking My Father for the gift of their lives.

"Please tell all of My people you can reach that abortion, pornography, incest, fornication, lying, stealing, cheating must stop!! Your country has become a nation of thieves, and beasts roam the streets preying on innocent victims. A new plague will be visited upon My lawless ones who think no one sees. A new devastation will wreak havoc among the cities already weakened by floods, and spread panic across the country."

*"So stand fast with your loins girded in truth
clothed with righteousness as a breastplate, and
your feet shod in readiness for the gospel of peace.
In all circumstances, hold faith as a shield, to
quench all the flaming arrows of the evil one. And
take the helmet of salvation and the sword of the
Spirit, which is the word of God."*
[Ephesians 6:14-17]

THE END TIMES

Jesus: "The time for quiet reflection is nearly over, and action will fill the lives of My faithful ones. You will be busy at all hours of the day and night. It will seem like one very long day interspersed with short periods of rest. If no support is given to certain age groups, soon it will come to pass that all age groups are at risk, who stand in the way of the progressive forces in the world. Oh My dear, dear ones, please come and pray before Me for your country. It will be so devastated before long. Changes will be in place in the world, the power wielded by those who come in and take over. The numbers of people who just disappear will alert you to the seriousness of the situation. By now, the troops in different parts of your country are prepared to attack at a moment's notice. You will see bloodshed like this country has never known. It will be many years before there is a return of peace, and the world will be decimated by then to an incredible degree.

"The hearts of My beloved followers will be broken, and you must gather them *into your arms and assure them of Our love.* It will be a huge endeavor on your part to convince them of this in the face of so much chaos and ruin. *Only patient love will reach through their sorrow* and, in many cases, *outrage.* When they are emptied and lonely, they will be better able to listen. In preparation for the time when you no longer have Me on your altars, fortify yourself with My strength and beauty contained in this great gift of My Father, (Jesus in the Blessed Sacrament). Thank Him, My children. Praise Him and adore His Majesty, as we wait together for the hour to strike.

"All is in readiness. Devastation and destruction are soon to be the norm. Spend all your time in the light, while time and light remain. There is joy in heaven over the good that will come out of the destruction and cleansing. As the light dims, you will need to remain even closer to the Light of Christ in order to see the truth and live it.

"After My Mother's appearances all over the world have come to an end, great doubt will enter the hearts of many believers (in the world.) It will be a time of heightened confusion, and the enemy will use this time to deepen those doubts and throw people into a panic. Appeal to their common sense and sense of balance. Call them back to reason and a sense of truth and security. Defend My Mother and My Presence in the Eucharist with words of love and logic, with thoughts of My promises, recalling all I have done for My people and how I am a God Who keeps His promises to lead My children out of the desert into the promised land.

"I am your Lord and God, Jesus Christ, Who reigns forever. My Flesh is given for the life of the world. When you see the Abomination of Desecration on My Altar, know that all will be accomplished very quickly to the end of this Era. Time has run out for all delays of My Father's Plan. Please spend what time is left with Me, your Supreme Commander and Chief! The Army of Heaven marches to the Battle in legions for the great confrontation between good and evil. The forces of Heaven will win, but the struggle will be fierce, My people.

"All of My Mother's Army waits for the first sign to be given to galvanize into action. The Day of the Lord, My children, is here for all to behold. I speak these words to you to calm your heart so that when events begin, you will be strong and calm in the face of so much chaos. Please confess your sins each week. Stay recollected in Our Presence with the Angels and Saints. This is the world in which your life can be lived out. These can be your companions for the remainder of your journey. Call on them, My dear ones, thank them, love them and know that this love is deeply felt and returned by all of them. Even those who then turn against Me will hold the truth deep in their hearts and have another chance at salvation.

"The prayers and great works of My chosen ones will work miracles in the lives and hearts of My poor, weak, lost, lonely children. It will be a time of redemptive prayer and suffering for all of you for all of them!! Know that we shall be victorious when the Day of the Lord arrives! Remember that I am always with you."

Blessed Mother: *"Before My Son returns, this world will be purified. People will be tried for their faith, and only a* *remnant will remain faithful to God. This will help to purify those who turn away from God in order to save their lives. All people will live in danger and fear, and think only of how to survive this great time of holocaust. Those faithful to Me and to Jesus will be protected in My Mantle until the time comes for His return. Some of your number will be brought to heaven to pray for those remaining on the earth. You will be sorely tried and severely tested in all of your endeavors, but you will overcome them as long as you remain close to My Son and me at every moment. If you will surrender yourself totally to the Father's design for your life, you will feel total peace and constantly praise Him Who has created you and knows what is best for you. My dear ones, give thanks to the Father for all that is, and you will be filled with joy and a surrender you have not experienced before. You know the meaning of these words, but it is time to put them into practice.*

"Know, my dear ones, that Satan is gathering many more to his camp and filling them with assurances of power and victory. These beliefs incite men to even greater acts of rebellion against authority. It will be a time of much confusion, as Our people wonder what is truth and which way to turn. The ability of those who attempt to lead will be greatly impeded by the power of evil present in the world and, especially, within My Church. The Day of the Lord has begun and all of Scripture is being fulfilled, as it was written. Discover that nothing is as important to you as the time spent in greater communion with My Son and His desires and words for you. This now, is paramount in your preparation.

"My dear ones, you would not believe all the secret plans that are in place to dominate the world by those who are enemies of God and His Church. These final graces will do nothing to help those hearts already filled with so much hatred. Crimes against Our children everywhere cannot continue to go unchecked by the justice of God Who will only be acting to protect His chosen people from the crimes of the evil one and his cohorts, his instruments of destruction on the earth.

"Each of you, who has been faithful, has nothing to fear, for protection is yours within My Mantle. The youth who belong to Me will be preserved for the future Church in order for it to continue to flourish. The golden age of peace and purity, that is about to become a reality during the Triumph of Our Two Hearts, will be filled with those who persevere to the end."

> *"So be imitators of God, as beloved children, and live in love, as Christ loved us and handed Himself over for us as a sacrificial offering to God for a fragrant aroma. Immorality or any impurity or greed must not even be mentioned among you, as is fitting among holy ones, no obscenity or silly or suggestive talk, which is out of place, but instead, thanksgiving. Be sure of this, that no immoral or impure or greedy person, that is, an idolater, has any inheritance in the kingdom of Christ and of God."*
> [Ephesians 5: 1-5]

UNITY

Blessed Mother: *"These are days of waiting for everyone, and you can pray for each other's patience and perseverance better as you experience these needs yourself. Spend your days in greater union with Our Two Hearts and the Father's Will for you. Much wisdom is being poured out by the Holy Spirit upon all those who will accept it. Many special signs are being given to Our faithful ones everywhere. The world waits for the Father to act in specific ways and often misses the signs He is actually giving!*

"Please, dear ones, be aware of your brothers and sisters everywhere, who suffer greatly and have far less of the world's goods to give them any comfort. The love that fills your hearts, Our love, that makes your hearts swell and your spirits sing can never be taken from you, even though you one day may lose all other possessions. Great will be the peace and protection for all those who live in

this manner. This is living in the Father's Will, little ones. This is surrender, the abandonment of all you hold dear for the Lord's sake, for His honor and glory and the good of all the people in the world. Live as though nothing else existed now, save Our Presence with all the Angels and Saints, for that is truly living in the Kingdom.

"Life always continues after a person dies. However, persons continue to live and grow and learn and develop in new ways. People continue their association with others, but in a whole new way of being and interacting. You will do this, my dear ones, as you more and more surrender to being more deeply committed to God's Will each step of the Way.

"The salvation of all My faithful children of My Army has been assured. It will be they who lead all Our lost ones back to the one flock and one Shepherd. They are aware of this and are ready to engage the enemies of My Son and His Church. Your own knowledge of the importance of obedience will greatly help them to understand with clarity how much this virtue is necessary to salvation. Without obedience to the Will of God, Our people are like loose bearings in a machine. It runs this way and that without proper control and often ends in a crash.

*"Please, avoid spiritual 'accidents', My children, by becoming more obedient to the Commandments, the Beatitudes, the Mercy that is being set before you daily. To **be a child of God**, one must **practice being childlike** and **dependent on the Father's care**. One must **trust that He will provide** all that is needed in that life, all the while **praising** and **thanking** and **listening** to the Father.*

Do Whatever Love Requires

"The lives of Our people have become much too complicated. While progress is a good thing, they were not meant to move at such speed, to focus on their own abilities the way it happens today. Your world has become consumed by noise and motion and a false idea of freedom. The evil one has enticed too many of Our youth with the glitter and 'possibilities' of a corrupt world. First the glitter and corruption must be destroyed. An appreciation of His gifts must return to the deepest core of individuals. This can only happen when they are deprived of any comforts and excesses.

"Dear ones of My Immaculate Heart, My Son talks of unity and love. This must be before there is any kind of peace. Listen to Him. He is the Truth and the Way that will take you to the Eternal Light. There must be a unity among my children, as well as within my Church. There is no longer time for egos, for pride; only time for love to unify all my children, all Our apostolates and groups into one Body of believers; all working for the Kingdom. Come now and follow me under my banner: The Two Hearts of Love and Mercy. Peace will reign as will hope, love and joy through the trials and tribulation that are ahead if there is unity of purpose and hearts. Trust! Trust in true humility of heart. Be love! Show love.

"Living in this world in this manner IS to be an instrument in the hands of My Son. As all of you continue to watch these events unfold, you will be guided by the Spirit in a greater way. You will know what to do and how to proceed, if you listen intently for His voice. I will always be with you praying for your needs. The love in your hearts

will continue to grow. Please always believe in the fact that you will be protected in my Mantle of love. Go in peace for now and please continue to hold my hand, my dear, dear ones."

Jesus: "Dearest ones, Mary, My Mother, is calling all to unity in one Body under My Headship. My Sacred Heart will reign soon, but you must first go through trials and tribulations. There is much unrest and unholiness in the world, much dissent and much pride. All My children must now bond together in peace and work together. There must be no division in My ranks. You are all serving the same God. You are all striving for your eternal reward, so I ask you please to work together as it was always meant to be. Many have created division, jealousies, dissension and apostasy. It is now time to come back and unite under the mantle of My Mother. Convert while there is still time."

STRENGTH

Jesus: "My dear ones, the advent of My Second Coming into the world is bringing with it many attacks of the evil one and his cohorts. I, your Jesus Who loves you and all His faithful ones, tell you that now is the Day of My Visitation to the hearts of the world. The world is full of dangers and deceits, little ones. None of you is strong enough to withstand the virulent attacks against your weaknesses. The only way for Me to protect all My children is for them to come away with Me in safety. The wiles of the evil one are no match for you.

"There is no way for you to withstand the advances of his plots and schemes against those who love Me and My Holy Mother. A day will not go by during which you will not need all of My strength, all of My help and grace...no matter where you are! Believe Me, little ones, the hour is upon the world for all the forces of evil to be loosed.

"All is about to unfold in your presence. All is about to become a state of extreme emergency in the world and in the heart of each one. The battle looms fiercely over-head. Feelings of oppression and distraction result from the major events in Satan's plan to conquer the world. They are appearing on the horizon as the world still sleeps. Only the graces granted by My Mother will see you through each event.

"This is by the Will of My Father for all of you. But you cannot avoid feeling oppressed and sad by the terrible carnage which awaits the world. The Angels and all the Saints are praying for you at each moment."

PERSEVERE

Jesus: "It will be necessary for all to have the greatest faith in all of Our promises. The power of My Father to save His world and His people is absolute and will not be overcome by any other power! The time allowed the evil in this world to increase *has been allotted by My Father to cleanse the earth and hearts* of all. When the amount of evil has reached the appointed measure, the love of My Sacred Heart and the power given to My Mother will burst upon the world to defeat all who stand in the way of the Triumph of Our Two

Hearts. Until then, all will need all of the strength and grace We have to give you in order to persevere.

"My people, new plans for the world are escalating the Father's justice in order to cleanse His people. The evil and slavery intended for this country is most appalling. The harm which will be visited by the enemies of the Church and freedom can only be lived and withstood with the help of My Mother and Myself, with all the Angels and Saints to rally around you in prayer and protection.

"Be aware of the opportunities for this protection. Ask for help at every moment. This is the only way all of you will survive and continue to persevere through the dark, dreadful times ahead. The delays are meant to strengthen you and test your resolve, your commitment and love for Us.

"THE TRINITY OF GOD IS GIVEN GLORY, HONOR AND PRAISE EACH TIME YOU ARE OBEDIENT, EACH TIME YOU DEFER TO THE WILL OF THE FATHER, EACH TIME YOU GRACIOUSLY AGREE TO WAIT JUST A LITTLE LONGER FOR HIS WILL TO BE DONE IN YOUR LIFE. MUCH FAITH IS NEEDED TO JUSTIFY THE MANY WHO WILL RETURN TO US AT THE VERY LAST MOMENT.

"You can see how you will all be victims for their sakes, and must accept this with joy, if you truly wish to serve your brothers and sisters. They will have no one else and no other way to have the graces reserved for them released. You must unite your sufferings with all of those in the world who are experiencing pain and hardships because of natural disasters, wars and poverty. Your prayers for them will release more graces at this time when they are most needed.

Choose for Me. Choose the love that no one else can give
you. My love is all you will ever need, My dear people, for
complete protection: complete fulfillment of every need,
every wish, every desire."

Chapter Eight

The Day of The Lord Continued

MEDITATION FROM OUR BLESSED MOTHER

"My dear people of My Immaculate and Sorrowful Heart, today is such a special one in your life and mine. Today we stand on the brink of a new era, consecrated and committed totally to the Divine Will of Our Father in Heaven. You are all so very dear to My Heart, my dearest little ones. I am so in love with each of you with a tender mother's heart. Please know, my children, that we are closer together now than we have ever been before.

"By a special grace and supreme act of His love, the Father is allowing me to come into your world and be seen by many of His special messengers. Because of the imminence of the Millennium, and the Second Coming back to the world of my dear Son, Jesus Christ, He has allowed me to be present to many and to speak as I am doing now, to very many of my faithful children, so that you may all benefit from my words of warning and love and preparedness.

"When you are expecting an important guest, especially one of your acquaintances, you clean your house and prepare the finest foods you can afford to purchase. Nothing is too good for this dignitary, and the arrival of this important person consumes all of your time and en-

ergy. If this person is delayed in arriving, you make every effort to maintain the status of the house and your level of preparedness. The delay is really no inconvenience because you are aware of the importance of this guest spending time with you in your very home! Whatever is needed to make this a most special occasion is uppermost in your mind and nothing can dampen your enthusiasm, or distract you from your plans. Is this not truly the way it is, my children?

"Well, my dear ones, my Son is about to return to the Earth. Just as I prepared myself and everything necessary to bring the Babe into the world the first time in Bethlehem; So now the Father is sending me to you to prepare you to receive Him. He is this most important dignitary. He is the God-Man Who will come to fight against all the forces of evil that will be gathered. He will save the world once again, as He stands in terrible array, surrounded by His Angels and all the Love and might of Our Heavenly Father! The Holy Spirit will fill all of you with the love and strength He brings in order to greet Him on that glorious day.

"Oh my dearest ones, can you not see that it will be the love of my Son that will be the cause of the great victory for justice and the peace of my Son, my Jesus? Please, my dear dear ones, believe that He is coming. Prepare your houses, your souls, to receive Him into the world. Be ready now to see Him stand before you. The victory of good over evil will be real, will be complete, my children. Prepare the finest foods for the celebration. Dress your souls in the finest array of colors (graces), the odor of holiness and

the joy of gladness and rejoicing. This will be my darling children! Prepare and rejoice with your Mother.

"Attend to your garments and stay close to me, as We make the final plans. A new Heaven and a new Earth are about to be made a reality. When you feel fatigue or doubt or fear, please call on my Angels and myself. We are with you all the time. Believe that we are here with you ready to protect and help you to prepare. Whatever happens in the meantime will be the results of the Father's love and mercy for all. Do not worry about yourselves. Just remember, the King of Glory is returning to secure a victory for each of you.

"Return now, little ones; bathe yourselves in the waters of grace and forgiveness. Dress yourselves with my virtues and the gifts of the Holy Spirit, my Beloved Spouse. Adorn your heads with rejoicing and sing songs of praise and thanks to the Father. Wait in humble service to your brothers and sisters, so that all may be ready when my Jesus returns. Rejoice with me, my beloved ones. The King comes to save you once again. I am your Mother who loves you. I praise the Father, my Son and Their Spirit in unity with all of Heaven and earth."

> *"Since you know very well that the Day of the Lord is*
> *going to come like a thief in the night. So we should*
> *not go on sleeping as everyone else does but stay*
> *wide awake and sober."*
> [I Thessalonians 5:2 & 6]

SECOND COMING OF CHRIST

Jesus: "Dear ones of My Sacred Heart, My Second Coming is imminent. The Triumph of Mary's Immaculate Heart is soon to come. Along with this will come the Reign of My Sacred Heart. All will be given a last chance to repent and proclaim My God-Head, for I am Christ The King. All must work now vigilantly for the coming Reign of My Sacred Heart and the Triumph of My Mother's Immaculate Heart. It will happen with or without your prayers, but with more of you praying and joining with Us in this final hour, there will be more unity of hearts and there will be more love. Please get as many as you can to join Us in these final hours. To join Us or not is the choice you will have. I respect, as does My Father, your free will, your choice, but dearest ones, think what the two choices are. Clearly they are: HEAVEN OR HELL. How can I put it more clearly? Start thinking with your hearts. Start trying to see the way I see, the way I feel and you will then know what must be done."

Blessed Mother: "*Beloved children, it is most important you have your hearts ready. Prepare them every morning and evening for His Coming because the time is near. Only the Father knows when. All of Heaven is preparing for it. I* *now tell you to seriously prepare, to wait and be ready for His Reign and for my Immaculate Heart to triumph. Your generation will see this. Do not put off repentance. There is no time to put off coming to God.*

"The Father had kept His promise to His people almost 2000 years ago for their release from bondage. He gave His only Son, the Eternal Word, to us lowly creatures so we too, as He had always meant, could once again share in His Eternal Life. There is much chaos and turmoil in your world and an ever increasing darkness encompassing mankind.

"This is tragic. Hold your tepid, indifferent brothers and sisters in your hearts. Please give them to me, to my Immaculate Heart where I will keep them in love and caress each as a special child of mine. Before you see this glorious happening of His Second Coming among you, Our God Who is so good must show His merciful justice because of His infinite love for His children. His Love will give man a chance to come into His arms and He will kiss you with a love like you have never known. What joy and grace you will be filled with when you come to Him. When the Father gives you the final opportunity of choosing Heaven (Him) or Hell (Satan), you will then have chosen your fate through your free will, your free choice. He will then invite you into His Kingdom or turn His back on you forever. I do not want to see one of you say no. The time has come for the most serious decisions you will ever have to make. The decision of an Eternity of happiness and love or an Eternity filled with tears and regret. Which will you choose?

"Children, my triumph is here and is continuing in hearts and souls who acknowledge me, and will continue being completed when a soul realizes who you are and

what you owe your Creator. In the fullness of time, in the new era, His Reign will come with my triumph and His glorious Second Coming will be felt and seen by all. His Second Coming will be triumphant and glorious. What joy my children will feel when they see Him in His glory after the turbulent times that preceded His coming. Sing in joyful rapture, for your prayers are to be answered soon. Scripture is to be fulfilled and happiness will abound. Be strong in faith and trust. Praise and thank Him for everything, for soon His glory will be known to all.

"The Most Holy Trinity has given Our beloved son, Pope John Paul, the vicar of Christ on earth and head of His Church the Body of Christ, a plan from the beginning of his Papacy. Pray with him and for him, as he knows of what We speak. Our children must support him in all he is asking and suggesting to the people of the world. All his writings and teachings should be taken to heart, learned, studied and then put into holy action, as all he does has been guided by the Holy Spirit at all times.

"Pope John Paul is a guiding light for all to follow

as he is directing you according to the plans of the Father towards the year 2000, which will bring dramatic change to your world as you now know it. Follow his plan for this preparation period going into the millennium year using the mercy of God as the prominent catalyst. These are important years before the year 2000. Stand firm in faith and in truth."

*"What will you do on the day of punishment, when
from far off, destruction comes? To whom will you
run for help? Where will you leave your riches."*
[Isaiah 10:3]

DARKNESS & LIGHT

Jesus: "Dearest ones, your concerns are well placed about all the unrest within My people. Satan will play upon the pride of each one as best he can with all his subtle cunning. There are not enough words to warn you all to prepare. Above all, these are allowed by My Father to strengthen you by pointing out your particular areas of weakness. He can bring good out of every situation and therefore, will allow you all to be tried in particular ways so that you might learn important lessons. These new understandings gird you for the future when temptations will be greater and graces less available to all.

"The darkness of the soul will invade all of you, and choices will seem more and more difficult. It will be then that a focus on My Face and all you know to be true and holy will be the only means of defense against the forces of evil. As you attempt to hold out, please remember the ultimate goal of Heaven for all Eternity. Remember the aid and actual presence of the Angels and Saints. Recall all the times We have promised you Our strength and protection. Believe in this, My beloved children.

"Please remind each one that you are never alone for a moment, that trials will be the stepping stones into Heaven, that each step has been smoothed first by Our footsteps walking before you. The feelings of love and comfort and joy will seem to lessen for a time, also. This is so you will all struggle to remember and have faith in all Our words. To have this kind of trust will bring light into your souls and be the sounding board for all Our dear lost ones who come to tell their stories. Your own trust and hope will be a beacon, My people, an impetus for the faith of all who seek.

"There will be little light left in the world ... only from within the hearts of My faithful ones in order to show others the way back to My Father. I will be that Light, My dear ones. I will be the Answer to all the questions ever posed to each of you. I am the Way, the Truth and the Light. I will be your salvation at every turn. I will be the One Who saves on every occasion. Do not fear to hope in complete protection at every moment.

"The adversary has no power like that of his Creator. He has no ability to defeat Our purposes or the Will of My Father in Heaven. Even though all will seem lost, you may trust against all odds, all appearances, that We will be victorious at just the right moment of the fullness of time. Rejoice, My little ones, the Kingdom is about to be revealed for all to see and choose. These times are like no other, and will convince so many of the truth of all the words spoken by My Mother all over the world. The Triumph of Our Two Hearts has begun. I call each one to be My beacon and live My love and My words for all.

"My dear ones, wrapped in the mantle of My Mother, trust and confidence will be the climate protecting you from the storms. The enemy will lie in wait for you and appear when you least expect it. You have only to call upon the power of My Name to deal with him. The attacks of the evil one will result in greater strength for the time period that will follow them. My Father's Plan will continue to require only your 'yes' and ongoing cooperation.

"Just have a deep conviction of love, My little ones, a total confidence in My love and care for you. This will be your peace. This will give you victory at every turn. This will fulfill the Father's Will for you and for His people. Live in My peace, children. Live immersed in My Love. To see clearly the state of the sinfulness existing in each soul will cause many of Our loved ones to panic. Our people are simply not aware of the sinful patterns in their lives. This revelation will be a source of bitterness and great sorrow *to many of Our chosen ones, as well.* My Father has accomplished so much good in His faithful ones by delaying His hand."

Blessed Mother: "*Each time you feel panic begin to invade your being, stop! Refocus on My Son, Jesus and Myself. Ask to be reunited to Our Hearts, and be allowed to concentrate again on truth and the reality of all that is. Each must make a choice, a step towards God in order to prevent major devastation. Please, continue to thank and praise Our Father Who loves you all so very much. Let us praise God Our Loving Father together now, My littlest ones. Be filled with joy and peace.*

"*Please children, seek comfort and refuge in my arms. Know that My Jesus and I long to hold and caress and comfort you. Love is the answer, and the peace of my Son awaits all who come to Him. It is important that you con-*

tinue to seek My Son and His love. This love will be a healing balm for your soul, and will strengthen you for the time to come. This love is a precious gift meant for all who seek it. Tell Our little ones about this love, and that this one gift is the only one they will ever need. I will help them to find My Son's love if only My children ask Me.

"The love of My Son is always there for all to share. It is this love which will conquer the evil one. In fact, this love of Jesus is the strongest gift from the Father and will keep the evil one from devouring Our children. It is this love which shall conquer in the end all of the evil which exists in the world today, and will ultimately soothe and appease the Father's wrath. This wrath is justice. This wrath will cleanse the world as it is meant to be cleansed, leaving it pure and white as snow. The love of My Son is the most powerful force on earth! Please ponder these words. You must believe them completely. I am your Mother Who loves you. Hear My plea!"

"Happy those who do what is right, whose deeds
are always just. Remember me, Lord, as you favor
your people; come to me with your saving help,
That I may see the prosperity of Your chosen,
rejoice in the joy of Your people, and the
glory of Your heritage."
[Psalm 106:3-5]

PURIFICATION

GOD THE FATHER: "It is I, your Heavenly Father Who
speaks to you. I am the God and Father of all, the Creator
and Redeemer, the Lover, the Friend, the Great Counselor,
the One and only Gift Giver for all Eternity. It was I Who
formed you in your mother's womb and knit you in darkness, so that one day you would serve Me and all My people
by doing special tasks which will aid the salvation of man.

"How I love My people and long to give them all My
gifts. They must return to Me in repentance, and I will
welcome them with open arms. The truth of My words
will become apparent to you, as all of this is accomplished.
Your world is about to be purified by Me for the great coming of My Son back into the world to lead all of you into
My land of promise and plenty. This time it will be Jesus,
My Beloved Son, Who leads you into the land flowing
with milk and honey, where former enemies will lie down
in peace together and all will live their lives in harmony,
praising their God and loving each other!

"Great will be the peace which you will experience
once the Day of the Lord is done, and I have visited My

justice and rid the world of evil. Great will be the rejoicing, and songs will reach to the highest heavens. We will feast together one day in My Kingdom forever, and all of your sadness and tears will be wiped away. No more will your heart be heavy with remorse and sorrow. No more will the weight of sin pull you down. No more will you need to be healed, for I Myself, will heal you and carry you into My Kingdom.

"The rejoicing of all My people will raise the joy in heaven to new heights, and laughter and love will fill all those gathered to praise and adore the Living God Who has saved His people, once again, from the power of the evil one. No more will he torment My beloved children. No longer will they weep and mourn, for peace and prosperity will fill the land. My people will be Mine forever!"

Jesus: "My people, the beauty and light of My Father's world is about to be extinguished by the prince of darkness and his cohorts. It is not possible to tell you how much suffering will exist in those days. In every instance of injustice, the world turns its back with indifference to the cruelties which exist. You are seeing these things because Satan is being allowed to play out his plan to destroy the earth step by step. There will be no peace from now on, My little ones, until after the Day of the Lord when the earth will be shaken from its foundation and wander aimlessly out of control. Then will the forces of evil be fully unleashed to cleanse the earth. All who deny Me shall be denied by Me! All who have thought to deceive Me shall see the truth of their actions. All who deceived My faithful ones shall be put to flight by My avenging horde. They shall be cast into hell forever! This must be...to rid the earth of evil, to cleanse it and prepare it for My coming again.

"It will unfold one step at a time, as it is already unfolding. When you see the Son of Man coming from on high, know that the hour is nigh! But before that time, there will be huge earthquakes. The earth will be rent by the violence of its shaking. There will be war which will devastate further this once great country of yours which has been sold by the hands of greedy men who care nothing for the welfare of mankind, but only care to fill their own bellies. In the days to come, not a building will be left standing. After a period of darkness, the earth will quake and all that is not of Me will perish, except for a few who will be allowed to remain by the Will of My Father. The Antichrist will be among these. He will bide his time until the moment when all will be proper for him to appear. This will signal the stage to be set for My Coming. At that time, you will know that I am very, very near.

"The great battle on the Day of the Lord will occur between the forces of evil and My own chosen people. Then I will come on a cloud with My Angels surrounding Me, and We will defeat Satan and his cohorts and they will be chained in the bowels of hell for a very, very long time. Then will I live and reign with you, among My people, in the beauty of the world as the Father intended it to be. There will be no pain, and joy and laughter will echo throughout the land. Already I am writing My Name on the foreheads of My beloved ones who will live with Me in a purified world. Then we will see and live out all that

Scripture has foretold, the promises of Yahweh and the promises given by Me. All who live will see the saving power of God! All who dwell on this earth will see My Coming in glory on that great day. I am anxious for this, My dear ones, as I have waited for time to reach its fullness, and a new time, a new era of peace and happiness will begin. I put My trust and hope in you. Please, dear ones, put your trust and hope in Me."

Blessed Mother: *"My children, the hand of God is about to fall. For thousands of years He has warned His people to return to Him in repentance. Now He will no longer wait for a hard hearted creation! He lowers His arm in great sorrow in order to cleanse the earth and fulfill all that Scripture has foretold. My Heart overflows with sadness and pity for the millions who will die and for the many millions who will remain to suffer in their grief. Bring them to me and, together, we will take them to My Son to be healed and cleansed of sin. The Lord, God, is waiting with open arms to take them back and nourish them back to health. The sickness of your day is a result of a lack of God in lives given over to earthly pleasures without the love of God to sustain the health of mind and soul. Great care and tenderness await all those who seek the love of God. Praise be to God Who is and was and always will be. IN LISTENING, YOU WILL BE LED. IN ANSWERING, YOU WILL BE PROTECTED."*

*"But the Lord keeps faith: He it is Who will
strengthen you and guard you against the evil
one. In the Lord we are confident that you are
doing and will continue to do what we enjoin.
May the Lord rule your hearts in the love
of God and the constancy of Christ.*
[2 Thessalonians 3:3-5]

TRANSFORMATION

Jesus: "My beloved children, the great trumpet is about to
blow throughout your land. Please child, read and meditate on Isaiah chapters 24, 25, 26 and 27. This book of
Isaiah was written centuries before I came to earth and
should be taken seriously in this your age. It is a prefigure-
ment of what will befall My children if hearts remain hardened to My Word, hearts that remain closed to the working
of My Spirit within you. It would be wise for you to take
seriously, once again, these words found in these chapters
of Isaiah which are apocalyptic. Please meditate on the
words found here, calling on the Holy Spirit to enlighten
your minds and hearts to know what the meaning is for
you in this present age. Then pray to know and understand
what it is you are being called to do.

"It is now your choice whether to change or not, to see
My Light or not, to follow Me or not, dear ones. These are
your choices. How you choose will determine your fate
and your future. So it would be wise to remember to live
today as you are being led, leaving the tomorrows to Me,
as I have planned for each of you. Then put the yesterdays

where they belong, in the past. Do not open yesterday's day. Open only today's door, the door that leads to Me, to your joy and the fulfillment of your every need.

"If you choose not to follow My Light and teachings, so be it. It is your freedom to do so. But be made aware of what lies in that decision of yours, of that direction you choose to take. You will no longer be able to say, 'I did not know,' as My Words are written through the prophets, disciples and apostles and were all divinely inspired by your God through the working of Our Holy Spirit Who dwells in all souls and hearts in the degree with which He is welcomed or is not welcomed.

"Remember, My little ones, you are all Temples of the Holy Spirit. Bring Him closer to you each day as He inspires you and then do as He inspires. Listen carefully in the quiet and the stillness of your hearts, otherwise you may miss your opportunity that could be of great and grave importance to you.

"Soon all will see, as I have foretold in past generations and in this generation, come to pass, and then I your Lord and God will wipe away all tears from your faces, as the veil will have been lifted and all will see My glory. You will then behold your God in all His glory as He has promised, for pride will have been banished from hearts for good. You will then dwell in the House of the Lord all the days of your lives, those who have followed, trusted and believed My Words. The table will indeed be spread by Me for each of you, as you come to receive your rewards in the House of your Lord. There will then be only joy and happiness for the rest of your days. (see Psalm 23)

"Dearest ones, you can do nothing about the events to come (because things have been set into motion) except to lessen their intensity through prayer, but you can do something important now about your souls. And this is what is important. You are not to trouble over what tomorrow will bring. Work on what We have planned for you today. As you work and live each day as I direct, as I Will, you will find the tomorrows will come easily and unfold in mysterious and wonderful ways. Focus on Me, on My love, on My mercy and how your prayers and your love can help this aching world of yours.

"The scales are tipping. Do not say to Me, "I will not serve". Lucifer would delight in taking more souls with him. I will not allow this and I want you not to allow it. You need to stand firm on faith, hope and trust. It is in and through prayer, even when you do not feel like prayer, that your spiritual strength will build, and a wall will be built around you by grace to be able to ward off the evil that wants to possess each of you. Do not let anything overshadow My Light. Come to Me to be nourished, to be fed by Me in the silence of your hearts, joining your hearts with Mine.

"You need this quiet. Come into the garden of My Heart where you will find the answers you need. I invite you to come each day and join your Fiats (yes) with Mary's in complete trust and love. You then will see miracles and transformations. Come now if you can, as much as two hours a day for adoration and prayer with Me, no matter what else you think important.

"Pray for conversions. Pray for your country's leaders. Pray they will change their hearts soon. How sad to live in a society where there are no morals or virtues left. So much depends on you, the few. I know the outcome, if more souls do not come back to Me and acknowledge God as the center of their lives. Pray as you have never prayed before. Your country and families need prayers like never before. Much faith, trust, perseverance and charity with complete unconditional love for each other will be needed. Your faith will be tested to its limit. It is better to believe when you have not seen.

"The next years are very crucial for souls. Many will be led away from Me, but many too, through your efforts of prayer and sacrifice, will be drawn into My mercy to see, live and know merciful love as it is. Along with the tribulations, trials and disasters which are escalating, you will see many extensions of mercy and love coming from all over the world in varied ways. I am not a vengeful God, but I AM A JEALOUS GOD. I must be first in your lives and I want you to love Me as I love you.

Pray for your brothers and sisters in Russia for their complete conversion. My children, My flower Russia will come once again into My loving Arms. There is hope. As with justice, there will be mercy. Peace will reign again and there will be joy in all hearts. Trust these words of Mine. Make yourselves available to be Our instruments and vessels of peace, of trust, of obedience, of humility, of charity, of love and of My mercy."

Blessed Mother: *"My dear, dear children, can you see, my little ones, how the natural disasters have been stepped up all over the world, as well as wars and diseases? There* is now so much apostasy in my Church, the Church My Son gave to all of you. It breaks my Heart. Please pray for my beloved Church and priest sons. I love them so.

"Live the Gospel, live according to the teachings of my Church and my loved son, John Paul, your Pope. Does not your Pope teach mercy and love? Listen to him. Obey him. Follow him. Pray for him. Love him. Your prayers, fasts, vigils, sacrifices will help things go according to Heaven's plan. This is a time of battle between good and evil. Call Jesus' Name often. Invoke St. Michael and His Angels and your Guardian Angels. The Rosary will be your weapon, as will the Scapular be your shield. Always wear blest objects. Satan hates the Rosary and the Eucharist. He will try to convince you it is not needed. Listen to me, your Mother, and always hold the Rosary. Then pray, pray, pray.

"I advise you not to be too hasty in making decisions, especially spiritual decisions, in these times. Much discernment is needed through prayer for everything. Beware! Stay within the folds of My Immaculate Heart and under the protection of my Mantle. I would ask you to read Matthew's Gospel, Chapter 13 and especially from verse 36. What do you feel the message is here? Know well these times are now being seen and felt in my Church. Those of mine who stubbornly go about sowing bad seed in my Church and to my sheep will soon find their just due.

"If you could see the pestilence and disease that will soon spread throughout all of Europe and the Continent. As waters subside, as buildings collapse, as crops are devastated beyond salvaging, there will be much hunger, much suffering, much horror and devastation that has not been *seen or felt like this before now. These are signs. Is anyone paying attention? There is grace and mercy for those who recognize, who believe and understand with the wisdom of the ancients. They will survive to help those who will wander from place to place, not knowing what to do or where and when to go.*

"There will come many who will seem most convincing. Do not change your focus. Keep looking straight ahead to the Cross and why He did what He did for each of you. Why the Father asked His only Son to do what was done for you. Do not lose sight of this now. Listen not to the many who will sound like prophets coming to show the way. Do not fall asleep. Each day continue to consecrate yourselves and everyone to Jesus through me. This is your only hope and this is the sign my Angels will look for. Your sign, the sign of my Heart on each of your heads and hearts, will counter the sign of the beast.

Many will say I did not know. YES, THEY DID! They have not listened. Many souls will be lost. Pray, sacrifice, fast and do good works! (Live Jesus and His Word.) Stay calm in joy and peace, no matter what, as I will always be with you. Even as My Son's mercy turns to His Merciful Justice, know that His mercy, His love will never run out and will never change for He never changes. He is infinite. Live what I have been telling you for so long. It is not too late to save many."

"My son, do not forget My teaching, let your heart keep My principles, for these will give you lengthier days, longer years of life, and great happiness. Let kindness and loyalty never leave you: tie them around your neck, write them on the tablet of your heart. So shall you enjoy favor and good repute in the sight of God and man."
[Proverbs 3:1-4]

THE ADVENT OF THE NEW MILLENNIUM

Blessed Mother: *"Dearest children, I have been taking all My children (His children), since He gave all of you to me, towards His Second Coming. By my teachings to many around the world, I have been leading all of you gently back to Him, to His Sacred and Merciful Heart. You are approaching the advent of the year 2000 commemorating the Incarnation of Jesus and His coming into the world as Savior and King. Because of my Fiat, my Yes when asked to be His Mother through the Angel Gabriel, I gave birth to the God-Man through the working of the Holy Spirit, my Heavenly Spouse. I have now been asked again in this century to take my children by the hand through my Heart and lead them into this New Advent, the coming of the Year 2000.*

"This will be a momentous occasion, as many will be drawn again to My Son, the Father and the Holy Spirit, the Most Holy Trinity. All in unified power will pronounce the coming of this New Advent, as I the Mother of Mercy (Who is Jesus, My Son), lead you, as the Mother and Queen of the New Advent. I am the New Eve and He, My Son, the

189

New Adam. We are asking all Our children to pray with Us for this coming event. Pray with Our chosen son, John Paul, as he knows what is to take place (by the year 2000). You are all being asked to prepare your hearts and your souls through a total giving of yourself to Jesus through me, as this is the only way you will be able to travel this road with Us into the new century.

"Many things are on the horizon. There is much hope and joy as all of Heaven is preparing with me, their Queen, to present your King once again to the world, to the hearts in which He will rule supreme. His reign is forever and is going to come through My Immaculate Heart, as I am the Immaculate Conception, the Bride of the Holy Spirit, Who guides and challenges all to come to Him now in all humility to imitate my virtues of obedience, trust, perseverance, humility, patience, purity. There is not a virtue of mine which you are not being asked to imitate.

"Much can be gained by coming every day in front of Him in the Blessed Sacrament or in Eucharistic Adoration and receiving Him in the Sacraments of the Eucharist and of Reconciliation. Then all guile, all pride, all anger, all ego, all self would be lost and only He would remain, would exist in each soul. It is then peace would reign in hearts, in families, in nations, in countries and in the world. So many scoff at this simplistic approach to peace, to joy, to a fullness with their God, their Creator, for many no longer believe in Him or are apathetic to Him and His teachings.

*"Through prayer all will realize again **His Real Presence** among men. They will realize love and mercy and how it is to be shared. The path to Heaven with Us in Eter-*

nity is rough and narrow, filled with suffering and sacrificing but also filled with hope and joy over the crosses He allows each of you to carry. You will be filled with praise and thanksgiving in this joy of your crosses. Empty yourselves completely so He can fill you with Himself and with the graces necessary to arrive at the next crossroads which is upon you. Much is yet to come before you come over that bridge from the mire into the new. Be watchful. Be prepared. Be in prayer. Be in the state of grace. Be in me and I in you, as I bring Him once more to all my children. Love, peace and joy make the difference. Pray with me always and never let go of my hand, as I will never let go of yours unless you ask to have me let go. Become as that little child, and I will lead you. As your trust grows, so shall your faith. Your self will die completely, as He lives more and more in you through me. Always live in my peace, love and mercy, showing that same peace, love and mercy to others, to yourselves and to your God. Do all for His honor and glory. I love you my children."

"His soul will live in prosperity, His children have the land for their own. The close secret of Yahweh belongs to them who fear them, His covenant also, to bring them knowledge."
[Psalms 25:13-14]

NEW EARTH

Blessed Mother: *"In the beginning of the world, when darkness and chaos ruled, it was a dreary and empty place. There was no beauty, no color, no loveliness of nature to brighten the dark places of the earth. There was only the sound of the wind and the rain. Oh, how it rained, with lightening and thunder to fill the air. It was necessary for the earth to begin like this because the forces of evil had already been let loose and were ruling the great chasm between heaven and earth. The difference was so great between Heaven and Earth so that Satan would realize all that he had lost by rejecting God for all eternity. There was much sadness in Heaven after the fallen Angels had been driven out of Paradise. There was no rejoicing except for the victory of Michael, the Archangel, who had defeated Lucifer. All the Angels were appalled at the sinful pride of the Angels who dared to follow Satan and refused to worship God.*

"This was the beginning of the worst kind of pride, the kind that refuses to serve, refuses to love. It was in this milieu that fallen Angels were cast into Hell and given dominion over the world. God, the Father, knew that He would create man, and it was at this time that He formulated all His plans for salvation. These included our first

parents who would sin and be cast out of Paradise be-cause of the sin of pride and disobedience. He, (the Fa-ther) knew this would happen and that the gates of Heaven would be closed until His Beloved Son would come upon the earth to reopen them. He loved His Son so dearly that He wished to reclaim mankind from all the harm and dam-age that would befall him in order to make a gift of them to the Son Who would then present them back to the Father, their Creator.

"He wished to create a suitable place for His people whom He loved and provide a beautiful world to give to His Son. It would be necessary to send His Son to redeem His people and restore a reign of peace. At this time, He saw all that would happen throughout history and, in that moment, His plans were formulated to save each age as it came near to total destruction, instead of learning to love and serve their God and Creator.

"MY SON IS COMING AGAIN! Know and believe this is true. Therefore, the Earth must be cleansed in order for Him to fulfill Scripture before He returns. All that is prom-ised in Scripture will occur. All of you will be participants in these great events. I have told you this short version of the story of the world, so that you will understand that Sa-tan is warring against the Father's plan to save His chil-dren and return the Earth to its former beauty. Satan wishes to destroy the world and return it to the state of chaos into which He originally was cast. That is why sinful men who follow Lucifer wish only to destroy goodness and beauty and return to darkness. The forces of evil will not stop until they are completely destroyed by God at the appointed time.

"Now is the time for the Triumph of My Immaculate Heart to begin, as the darkness becomes nearly complete. Without the Mother, a child is lost and uncertain which way to turn. Without the touch of her hand, the heart grows colder and the heart is hardened from all that assails it in this world. There is no comfort like that of a mother. There is no joy like that of a mother beholding her children at play, at rest, learning and growing in the virtues of goodness. I will defeat the evil one with my cohort of Angels, my heavenly Angels, and my earthly angels who love me and have given their lives to my cause. A new heaven and a new earth are about to be born out of the birth pangs of the world. O Alien world, you have drifted far from the path of salvation and have become a foreigner in your own land. You are not aware of your birthright, purchased for you by My Son.

"All is about to be purified and rendered clean in the sight of God. Then it will be deemed worthy to present to the Son upon His return. The Son will, in turn, take all to His Father, and They will rejoice together over your and their good fortune. Happy are you who will see this day. Give praise to Our Father Who so loves the world that He will send His only Son, again, to save His people and bring all to the completion of this Age.

"THE FUTURE OF ALL WHO PRAY IS BRIGHT WITH THE LIGHT OF CHRIST, MY SON. BE FILLED WITH JOY, AS WE WORK TOGETHER FOR THE GOOD OF MANKIND. BE FILLED WITH GRATITUDE TO THE FATHER FOR ALLOWING THIS EXTENDED TIME OF GRACE."

"Though I pass through a gloomy valley, I fear no harm; Beside me Your rod and Your staff are there, to hearten me. You prepare a table before me under the eyes of my enemies; You anoint my head with oil, my cup brims over. Ah, how goodness and kindness pursue me, every day of my life; My home, the house of Yahweh, as long as I live."
[Psalms 23:4-6]

CHOOSE

Jesus: "I am the Lord, your God, Who was and Who is and Who will always be. Be immersed in My love forever more, My people. Be one with My Heart, with My Spirit, with the Will of Our Father in Heaven. Be at peace, secure in Our Two Hearts. The Father continues to grace the world, even as it continues to reject Him. No one can imagine the immense amount of love He has for His people.

"Human ability to love and forgive and tolerate each other's behavior is barely a shadow of the Father's ability to do so. But this has also given way to complacency in the hearts of all, a false understanding and taking for granted the continued forgiveness as a license to sin, to put off changing and living life as a child of God. It is this condition, a scheme of the evil one, which has lulled the world into an illusion of reality. Nothing of the world reflects the goodness of the Creator as it was meant to. Now, that beauty is about to disappear. The love and longing for His people's love is about to force the Father's Will into action. He will, once again, do what is necessary to reach the dull minds and hearts of all who sleep in the false security of the world. The Father is returning beauty to the world by first destroying all that is ugly, all that is not of Him, all the reminders of the evil one.

"Great **beauty and peace** will be the final result of all that is about to occur. It has been the Father's Plan at work all along for the preparation of as many of His children as will respond to Him. It is love and healing and mercy and forgiveness and new life He offers to a tired world nearly dead already in sin and debauchery. To dwell with Us in the present moment is the answer to being faithful and persevering. A **focus on My Mother** and Myself, present with each of Our chosen ones, will serve to bring each of you through impossible trials. These times and trials are necessary to accomplish all My Father has planned for His people. Trust is the only answer for all of you, My dear ones. The mood of many is to doubt. The evil one casts many aspersions, slander. The focus must be on Me, I tell you. There must be no place in your life for idle chatter and wonderings. The time left is too precious to waste on idleness and selfish chatter. Without people who persevere in prayer, many will not have a chance at conversion. Please, remember how much your faith will be a gift for Our poor children who continue to resist Our pleas. MUCH FAITH IS NEEDED TO JUSTIFY THE MANY WHO WILL RETURN TO US AT THE VERY LAST MOMENT.

"You can see how you will all be victims for their sakes, and must accept this with joy, if you truly wish to serve your brothers and sisters. They will have no one else and no other way to have the graces reserved for them released. You must unite your sufferings with all of those in the world who are experiencing pain and hardships because of natural disasters, wars and poverty. Your prayers for them will release more graces tat this time when they are most needed. Choose for Me. Choose the love that no one else can give you. My love is all you will ever need, My dear people, for complete protection, complete fulfillment of ever need, every wish, every desire. Please continue to be at peace."

UPON THIS ROCK

Blessed Mother: *"Please, continue to listen, My dear ones, to the voice of my Beloved Spouse. His Wisdom is all you need as a shield of protection, a weapon with which to defend all that you believe and know to be true. The truth is the ultimate weapon of defense against all* *the powers of hell. The love of Jesus is an adornment for your soul. The light of My Son will shine forth as a beacon to light the Way for all those seeking Him as a refuge. Please, prepare others. When the stone enters the pond, its ripples reach ultimately to the farthest shore. The action of the Holy Spirit, initiated by your reaching out to others, will go on and on until it eventually returns to nurture even yourself once again. The love and grace of My Jesus never stops overflowing onto all those who seek it and receive it with an eager heart. The Sacred Heart and My Immaculate Heart are your refuge, your home, your comfort, the place of renewal in times of need of renewal. All danger will be overcome, My little ones, when you flee to Our Hearts and receive the love and protection waiting for you there."*

GOD, THE FATHER: "Ask what you will, My beloved ones, and it will be given according to what is best for your souls. The souls of all My dear faithful ones are as gold gleaming in the Light of My Son, the Christ and Savior I have sent into the world. Only My Wisdom can determine the proper moment for the commencement of My Plan. These are My creation, and I act with the greatest love and mercy to prepare everything and everyone for the return of My Son. It is with great anticipation for His return that I begin even more to send special signs and wonders to the world. Be filled with longing for Me, My dear ones. Be filled with gratitude for My love for you, and go in the peace of My Will. I Am."

BE ENCOURAGED

Jesus: "I, your Jesus, praise My Father in Heaven. My only joy is to do His Will which includes loving all of Our people, all Our little ones, especially those who still refuse to come to Us in obedience. The day is here for the deliverance of the people of God from the slavery of sin and heresy. This day will continue to play out in all of your lives in different ways according to His Will for each of you. I, your sweet Jesus, tell you it is now.

"Tell all My people that from this moment on, they must be Mine alone, one in Our Spirit with My Will for all of their time and attention. This does not mean that you will abandon your duties, but that your focus is only on My love for you. The gifts My Father desires to give to each one can only be received in the closest union with My wishes for you and, My people, I desire that you receive every gift you need to equip you for the days ahead.

"Now is the final time of unity with Our Will. Each step you take must be in complete harmony with Our desires. The path you now tread will be the perfect way to My Father's Will and the perfection He wishes to give to you. This perfection is a docile and joyful living each moment in Our Presence. Knowing that We are accompanying you at every moment WILL carry you through each event.

"These trials will not be easy, nor anything you would normally choose, since the severity of testing will take you far beyond your normal limits of courage. Indeed, the ability of each one to fight evil on Our behalf will depend upon your openness to the Holy Spirit. You will fight and resist with Our strength and must rely totally on His help from now on. Instead of relying in the usual way on your own abilities no matter how great they seem to be, you can and must believe that We will never abandon you or leave you without the strength and perseverance you will need. My dearest faithful ones, this is so important. It will mean your very life and in some instances your very soul life!

"There is nothing, My people, that is more important for you now than a total living in union with your God and your holy and precious Mother. *All of Our words to you must form the fabric of your decisions.* Know in your hearts what is important now, and that is serving your brothers and sisters and being faithful to your God. The time for other projects and interests is long past. It is the time for strict attention to My Mother and her Angels. Stay closer than ever to her, My little ones, and listen to the soothing tones of her voice filled with love and concern for all of you, her dearest children. This is such a serious and real request from your Lord.

"Listen and respond with all of your hearts, My dear people. Come away with Me at every opportunity for prayer of quiet. These opportunities to close out the world and absorb My love will carry you through every obstacle the evil one seeks to place in your way. Learn more about My love, My dear people, by absorbing it in the silence. Sit before Me and gaze at My loving Heart. Adore Me in the hiddenness of My Sacrament before you on the Altar. Stay with Me now while I am still present here in your churches. Be in My Sacramental Presence while it is still available to you. Only this will build up a well of strength from which to draw for the hours of fatigue that await you. You will be filled with dread and even terror at times, as the enemy challenges everything that is sacred.

"My dearest people, know that the evil one will ascend to great heights now. The only recourse for My faithful ones will be total reliance on everything you have heard from My Mother and Myself. Rely on the Immaculate Heart and My Sacred Heart to be your refuge. That means fly to Us at every moment. Consecrate at every moment whatever you are doing. Your faith in Our protection and help will enable the utmost to be given. What you will see in the coming years will serve to strengthen your faith and see you through to the end or will cause My people to be reduced to fearful ones who give in to all the demands of the enemy. There will be no lukewarm response now. It will be either yes or no! Your ability to hold out in the face of even torture will be determined by the love you have for Us and the supreme value you place on Eternal Life for your soul.

"There is nothing, My dear ones, that is worth losing your soul to eternal damnation (for). Think of forever in the company of hate-filled souls suffering the torments of the damned. Let this image be your impetus to hold out until the end of life on earth. Let the promise of My love and the bliss of Paradise fill you with joyful expectations and conviction. My people, you are called to be happy for all eternity in the Kingdom of My Father, uninterrupted bliss and happiness. There are no human words to describe the greatness of the gifts of My Father. Be one with His plans for you, My people. Be a part of

His chosen remnant who stand firm in the face of suffering and deprivations.

"It will not be easy for you to hold out in the face of possible torture and even death. There cannot now be a turning away from all it means to be children of God. You are created to live My life in all its dimensions, My people, because you are created to receive the eternal rewards earned by My Passion and Death and Resurrection. All the graces you need are here for the asking, are yours for the taking, will be given in over abundance as you repeatedly turn to Us in complete trust. The joy you will have in living in this way will further convince you to persevere because you will know that it could only result from My Father's gift to you.

"Do not be afraid, My people. Nothing will happen to you and your families that is contrary to My Father's Will. Each one who is taken into Eternity will be brought before Him as just and merciful judge. I, Myself, am the One Who will guide each loved one into the Kingdom of My Father where they will pray for all of you in love and total peace and sublime happiness.

"These very, very serious times in the world must be attended by a new maturity and sense of devotion and commitment to personal sanctity and the salvation of all those We send to you. In the coming days when so many more will see the truth of their hearts and souls, each one will need to surrender totally the rest of their lives here on earth to the action of the Father's Will in each life and to accept instantly all of those who come as their fondest brother and sister and grave responsibility.

"All is too serious now to put off paying strict attention to each request, each call to all of you. You know in your hearts how needy and careless you were at one time, and without the gifts and graces being given, you would not be in the right place to continue to grow in love and service.

"Know that it is necessary to heal your hearts more completely so that families and groups of believers, that have been divided by the cunning of the evil one, can be restored whole and healthy without judgements and righteous attitudes! Many gifts are being poured out for Our people. Please pray that all will accept them immediately. Your prayers are the jewels which adorn your heavenly crowns, My dear ones. Prepare yourselves to approach the throne of My Father in gleaming finery!

"Open your hearts to receive all the grace and power you will ever need, My dear, dear ones. I love you with all the love that could be poured out for you. You can feel My love for you, if you will only stop and listen to My words to your hearts. Please believe these words, little ones. They are meant to save you. Come away and love."

Do Whatever Love Requires

Summation

REFLECTIVE THOUGHT

"The first response to Truth is hatred."
(St. Augustine)

Jesus Who is Truth, was hated so much for bringing the truth to mankind, hated so thoroughly that He was put to death by crucifixion. What is hatred but anger, resentment, mis-trust, animosity, dislike (especially if someone or something goes against what we think or feel) hostility and distaste?

What is my reaction, my feeling when someone tells me the truth about myself? Do I immediately resent it? Does this feeling of dislike well up in the depth of my being? Do I get angry at not only what has been said, but at the person saying it? Do I admit to the possible truth of what has just been said? Do I really admit to the truth of it or do I persist in glassing over the truth to suit my ego?

Do I like to condemn or think badly of others or criticize without accepting charitable criticism myself? Have I faced the realty that maybe I should change? Do I then take a long hard look at myself or do I lash back at the other person with a vengeance? What will be my reaction when I see myself as God sees me? Will I disbelieve what I am hearing or seeing about myself, as God sees me? Or will I immediately say, 'oh no, that's not me, this is just a trick?'

Will I resent God the Father for this; get angry with Him, or will I take a long look at what My Father, in His love and mercy, has just revealed to me about myself and then praise and thank Him for loving me so much, for caring enough about me to want to help me out of this ego trip, this pride, this false sense of self, my self centerdness and show me where I need to change?

Do I realize I cannot change until I repent? Do I want to change and repent? Do I want to ask for forgiveness of Him, of my brother or sister whom I have offended? Will I be a big enough person to swallow my pride and say, "I'm sorry, please forgive me"? Will I refuse to believe what has just happened to me? Will I say, "I do not believe this is real, this is happening"? Will I continue to say, "I will not serve?" Will I, by doing this prideful act, turn my back on Him, going away from Him instead of to Him?

These are the decisions I will have to make when our God, in His abundant grace, shows me the ultimate love and mercy in His Heart for me by allowing me to see myself for what I really am: *a sinner.* Will I make the decision to run to Him when He asks me, with His arms opened wide to me to come to Him, NOW?

What will I do in that split moment of time, a time that will not come again, when all of humankind is seeing themselves as God sees us? **What will you do? How will you respond to the TRUTH?**

CONCLUDING THOUGHTS

The following provocative thoughts were given on the Feast of Jesus' Baptism in the Jordan by a holy priest who meant for each of us to look back on our lives, who we are and why we were created, what being a "Christian" through baptism means to us, and what and how it differs from the Baptism of Jesus.

As Jesus was being baptized by John in the Jordan, the heavens opened and a voice spoke (which we know to be God the Father) and the Spirit in the form of a dove descended upon Him. The voice said, "You are My beloved Son. On You My favor rests." (Mark 1:9-11) This was the first time that the Three Persons in One God, the Trinity, was revealed to us. Jesus then accepted, though completely without sin, a baptism of repentance, thereby identifying Himself wholly with our humanity.

Our baptism differs from that of Jesus. Through baptism we are cleansed of sin and are baptized into a new Christ-like life which begins within us. We become "Christians" through our baptism by water and the Spirit, into the very life of God; our sins are completely washed away. We become His children by adoption through the merits of His Son Jesus' suffering, death and resurrection.

How do you identify yourself as a Christian? How do people identify you as a Christian? Do you love all people unconditionally? Do you harbor anger, resentments, judgments, criticize and condemn, even harm one of your bothers or sisters, or yourself?

NOTE: This is what Webster has to say about the word 'Christian':

> 1) declaring belief in Jesus as Christ and following the religion based on His teachings. 2) relating to or derived from Jesus and His teachings. 3) manifesting the qualities or Spirit of Christ. 4) relating to or typical of Christianity or its adherents. 5) one who lives according to the teachings of Jesus. To be Christ like, Webster further says: "having the spiritual qualities or attributes of Christ."

Is it your goal, is it mine, to live out the meaning of CHRISTIAN? How are we going to achieve this? Perhaps the words of **St. Margaret Mary** can shed some light on the way we must follow:

> "You should never find fault with, accuse, or judge anyone but yourself ... Never keep up any coldness towards your neighbor or else the Sacred Heart of Jesus will keep aloof from you. When you resentfully call to mind former slights you have received, you oblige Our Lord to recall your past sins, which His Mercy had made Him forget."

Prayer Appendix

THE HOLY ROSARY

The message of the Angel Gabriel "Hail Mary . . ." (or "Rejoice Mary" in the original Greek text) is a message of joy. Since the rose is a symbol of joy the sequence of 150 Hail Mary's by which we honor Mary and beg her intercession, is called the **"Rosary."** We pray 150 because there are 150 Psalms. From the earliest times it was the duty of priests and religious to regularly pray the Psalms. For lay-brothers, who could not read, it was the practice to pray 150 Ave-Maria's instead. During each ten Ave's they would meditate upon a mystery of the Faith. This is how the Rosary in its present form originated.

Usually one prays a third each day: five decades of ten Hail Mary's. On Mondays and Thursdays we pray the five **Joyful Mysteries:**

The Annunciation
The Visitation
The Nativity
The Presentation
The Finding

On Tuesdays and Fridays the five **Sorrowful Mysteries:**

The Agony in The Garden
The Scourging at The Pillar
The Crowning With Thorns
The Carrying of The Cross
The Crucifixion & Death

And on Wednesdays and Saturdays the five **Glorious Mysteries** which are the foundation of Christian life:

The Resurrection
The Ascension
The Descent of The Holy Spirit
The Assumption of Mary
The Coronation of Mary

After announcing the Mystery we begin each decade with the "Our Father" followed by ten "Hail Marys" and at the end of the decade the "Glory Be" in honour of the most Holy Trinity. This is followed by:

Oh My Jesus forgive us our sins, save us from the fires of Hell. Lead all souls to heaven most especially those in need of Thy mercy.

THE LITANY OF HUMILITY

The Litany of Humility (Source: Pieta Prayer Book)

O Jesus, Meek and humble of Heart, hear me..
From the desire of being esteemed...
From the desire of being loved....
From the desire of being extolled....
From the desire of being praised....
From the desire of being consulted.....
From the desire of being approved....
"Deliver me, Jesus"(to be said after each of above)

From the fear of being humiliated.....
From the fear of being despised.....
From the fear of suffering rebukes....
From the fear of being calumniated.....
From the fear of being forgotten....
From the fear of being ridiculed....
From the fear of being wronged.....
From the fear of being suspected....
"Deliver Me, Jesus" (to be said after each of above)

That others may be loved more than I.....
That others may be esteemed more than I....
That in the opinion of the world, others may in-
crease and I may decrease....
That others may be chosen and I set aside....
That others may be praised and I unnoticed...
That others become holier than I, provided that I
may become as holy as I should...
"Jesus, grant me the grace to desire it." (to be said
after each of the above)

NOVENA PRAYER TO SAINT ANTHONY
(Good prayer for conversion.)

Loving Saint Anthony

You always reached out in compassion
to those who had lost their faith.
You were especially concerned
because they had lost access to the
healing words of Jesus found in the
Sacrament of Reconciliation and in
the nourishing presence of Jesus
in the Sacrament of the Eucharist.

Intercede for _____
who has stopped practicing his/her faith.
Reawaken in his/her heart a love
for our Church and the sacraments,
and enkindle in his/her heart a sense
of forgiveness for the ways he/she
might have been hurt by members
of the Church who fell short of the
teaching of Christ.

Finally, St. Anthony, help me to
respond to my own call to conversion
so that I might become an example
of someone who has found great peace
in the arms of Christ.

May the joy I experience as a Catholic
be an invitation to those who are lost
to come home again
to the Church which we love.
Amen

Source: The Companions of St. Anthony, Conventional
Franciscan Friars, Saint Anthony of Padua province,
Ellicott City, MD.

SUGGESTED PERSONAL "ACT OF CONSECRATION TO SACRED HEART OF JESUS THROUGH THE IMMACULATE HEART OF MARY"

(From *Total Consecration according to Saint Louis Marie de Montfort* - Montfort Publications).

"I _____ a faithless sinner, renew and ratify today in thy hands the vows of my Baptism; I renounce forever Satan, his pomps and works; and I give myself entirely to Jesus Christ, the Incarnate Wisdom, to carry my cross after Him all the days of my life, and to be more faithful to Him than I have ever been before.

"In the presence of all the heavenly court, I choose thee this day for my Mother and mistress. I deliver and consecrate to thee, as thy slave, my body and soul, my goods, both interior and exterior, and even the value of all of my good actions, past, present, and future; leaving to thee the entire and full right of disposing of me and all that belongs to me, without exception, according to thy good pleasure, for the greater glory of God in time and in eternity."

SUGGESTED FAMILY CONSECRATION TO JESUS THROUGH MARY:

"Jesus, our most loving Redeemer, You came to enlighten the world with Your teaching and example. You willed to spend the greater part of Your life in humble obedience to Mary and Joseph in the poor home of Nazareth. In this way You sanctified that FAMILY which was to be an example for all CHRISTIAN FAMILIES.

"Graciously accept our(my) family which we(I) dedicate to You. Be pleased to protect, guard and keep it in holy fear, in peace and in the harmony of Christian charity. By conforming ourselves to the Divine Model of You Family, may we all attain to eternal happiness.

"Mary, Mother of Jesus and our Mother, by Your intercession, make this our(my) offering acceptable to Jesus and obtain for us graces and blessings.

"Saint Joseph, most holy guardian of Jesus and Mary, help us by your prayers in all our spiritual and temporal needs, so that we may praise Jesus our Divine Savior, together with Mary and you, for all eternity.

"Lord, we(I) pray that You visit our home and drive from it all snares of the enemy. Let Your Holy Angels dwell in it to preserve us in peace; and let Your Blessing be always upon us."

"Through the prayers of the Blessed Virgin Mary, we beg you to guard our family from all danger. As we humbly worship You with all our hearts, in Your mercy, graciously protect us from all the snares of the enemy and keep us in Your peace. We ask all this through Jesus Christ our Lord. AMEN."

Note: To consecrate means "To make holy and set aside for God's service." When you personally or as a family or for your family consecrate to Jesus through Mary, you are pledging and declaring that: "We are Yours and Yours we wish to be. This family (or yourself) will be at Your service. We(I) will return Your love for love. Your Heart(s) enthroned in our(my) home will be a reminder for us(me) and the model of our(my) love for one another."

RECOMMENDED READING

1. The Bible.
2. The Catholic Catechism.
3. Pope John Paul II Apostolic letter: *"Tertio Millennio Adveniente"* – Source: Daughters of St. Paul.
4. *True Devotion to Bl. Virgin Mary* – Source: Montfort Publications.
5. *Thoughts and Sayings of St. Margaret Mary* – Source: Tan Books.

ACKNOWLEDGMENTS

We thank all those who have helped put this booklet together, our families, especially our husbands for their patience, support and tons of love, and many friends. Special thanks to Fr. Bob, to Paul, our computer editor, to Angel Marion, to two special priests and one holy nun in the San Diego area. Most especially God the Father for allowing Jesus and Mary and the Saints speak to our hearts for His children. THANK YOU!